# THE DRAMATIC MONOLOGUE

## STUDIES IN LITERARY THEMES AND GENRES

Ronald Gottesman, Editor
University of Southern California

# THE DRAMATIC MONOLOGUE

Elisabeth A. Howe

Assumption College

Twayne Publishers
An Imprint of Simon & Schuster Macmillan
NEW YORK

Prentice Hall International
LONDON • MEXICO CITY • NEW DELHI • SINGAPORE • SYDNEY • TORONTO

Studies in Literary Themes and Genres No. 10

*The Dramatic Monologue*
Elisabeth A. Howe

Twayne Publishers
An Imprint of Simon & Schuster Macmillan
1633 Broadway
New York, NY 10019-6785

**Library of Congress Cataloging-in-Publication Data**
Howe, Elisabeth A.
    The dramatic monologue / Elisabeth A. Howe.
       p.   cm. — (Twayne's studies in literary themes and genres : 10)
    Includes bibliographical references and index.
    ISBN 0-8057-0969-x (cloth)
    1. Dramatic monologues—History and criticism.  2. American poetry—20th century—History and criticism.  3. English poetry—19th century—History and criticism.  4. Browning, Robert. 1812–1889—Criticism and interpretation.  5. Tennyson, Alfred Tennyson, baron, 1809–1892—Criticism and interpretation.  6. Eliot, T. S. (Thomas Stearns), 1888–1965—Criticism and interpretation.
7. Pound, Ezra, 1885–1972—Criticism and interpretation.  I. Title.
II. Series: Studies in literary themes and genres : no. 10.
PS309.D73H69   1996                   96–31199
821'.02—dc20                            CIP

10 9 8 7 6 5 4 3 2 1

Printed in the United States of America

For my parents
Winifred and Geoffrey Bailey

and for my children
Nicholas and Penny

# Contents

# Preface

The dramatic monologue has been the subject of much critical discussion in recent years. This book is intended as a guide to the genre for students and other interested readers, pointing out areas of disagreement, summarizing some of the arguments, and presenting, it is hoped, a balanced view of the dramatic monologue form. Representative poems by individual poets are analyzed, with a view to illustrating the various characteristics of the genre and its development over the years.

Most readers associate the dramatic monologue with Robert Browning. One can find examples of dramatic monologues in English poetry before Browning's time, though the genre was not recognized as such, but he certainly exploited and developed the form more than any previous poet. The first poem analyzed in detail here is Browning's "The Bishop Orders His Tomb at Saint Praxed's Church." Tennyson's "Tithonus" follows, as does a brief survey of dramatic monologues by other Victorian poets such as Algernon Swinburne, Christina Rossetti, George Meredith, Thomas Hardy, and Rudyard Kipling (see Chapter 2).

Chapter 3 examines the age of Modernism by looking at representative works by Ezra Pound and T.S. Eliot, who both wrote dramatic monologues in their youth and turned later to other forms. This chapter presents close readings of Pound's "Marvoil" and Eliot's "Portrait of a Lady," and explores the relationship between their dramatic monologues and those of Browning and Tennyson.

Chapter 4 begins with a survey of dramatic monologues by other 20th-century poets, especially E.A. Robinson, Edgar Lee Masters, Robert Lowell, and Randall Jarrell, and concludes with close readings of "A Servant to Servants" by Robert Frost and "A Pre-Raphaelite Ending, London" by Richard Howard.

The final section of the book offers an annotated bibliography of critical works on the dramatic monologue and on individual poets, followed by an annotated list of dramatic monologues by major practitioners of the form.

I am grateful to the NEMLA (Northeast Modern Language Association) for a Summer Grant in 1994, and to Assumption College for a Faculty Development Grant in summer 1993 and a course-load reduction in the fall semester 1994, all of which helped in the writing of this book.

I thank Ronald Gottesman, General Editor of the series *Studies in Literary Themes and Genres*, for much helpful advice. I would also like to express thanks to my friend Frances Knight, for her meticulous proofreading; to my friend Ann Waters, for pointing me in the direction of Richard Howard; and to my family, for their patience, support, and encouragement.

# Acknowledgments

I am grateful for permission to quote from the following works:

Excerpts from "Portrait of a Lady," "The Love Song of J. Alfred Prufrock," and "Burnt Norton" in *Collected Poems 1909–1962* by T.S. Eliot, reprinted by permission of Faber and Faber, Ltd.

Excerpts from "Portrait of a Lady" and "The Love Song of J. Alfred Prufrock" in *Collected Poems 1909–1962* by T.S. Eliot, copyright 1936 by Harcourt Brace & Company, copyright © 1964, 1963 by T.S. Eliot, reprinted by permission of the publisher.

Excerpts from "Burnt Norton" in *Four Quartets,* copyright 1943 by T.S. Eliot and renewed 1971 by Esme Valerie Eliot, reprinted by permission of Harcourt Brace & Company.

Excerpts from "1915 A Pre-Raphaelite Ending, London" from *Untitled Subjects* by Richard Howard reprinted by permission of Scribner, a Division of Simon & Schuster. Copyright © 1967, 1968, 1969 by Richard Howard.

Excerpts from *Collected Shorter Poems* by Ezra Pound reprinted by permission of Faber and Faber, Ltd.

Excerpts from *Personae* by Ezra Pound, copyright 1926 by Ezra Pound, reprinted by permission of New Directions Publishing Corporation.

# Chronology

This chronological survey of the dramatic monologue takes the works of Browning and Tennyson as its starting-point. It should be remembered, however, that earlier isolated poems can be classed as dramatic monologues even though the genre as such was not yet recognized. Examples include the Anglo-Saxon "Banished Wife's Lament," John Skelton's "Boke of Phyllyp Sparowe" (1508), Andrew Marvell's "Mower" poems (1681), Alexander Pope's "Eloisa to Abelard" (1717), and Joseph Warton's "The Dying Indian" (1740s). Toward the end of the eighteenth century, the form became more common: "The Negro's Complaint" by William Cowper dates from 1788; William Blake's "The Chimney Sweeper" and "The Little Black Boy" from 1789; and the last decade of the century gave us, among others, Blake's "The Nurse's Song," Housman's "The Carpenter's Son," Hardy's "My Cicely," Wordsworth's "Complaint of a Forsaken Indian Woman," Kipling's "McAndrew's Hymn," and Robert Burns' "Holy Willie's Prayer." Many dramatic monologues were written in the early nineteenth century, but mostly by minor poets; they were often melodramatic or maudlin in tone and did not develop the psychology of the speaker.

1832    Tennyson's *Poems* (dated 1833) includes
        "Oenone," practically a dramatic monologue,
        though with a short narrative introduction.

**1836** Browning publishes, in the *Monthly Repository,* the dramatic monologues that would eventually become known as "Johannes Agricola in Meditation" and "Porphyria's Lover."

**1842** Tennyson's *Poems* includes dramatic monologues "Ulysses," "Saint Simeon Stylites," "Tithonus," and "Locksley Hall." This collection is well received by the public and marks the beginnings of his success.

Browning's *Dramatic Lyrics* includes dramatic monologues "My Last Duchess," "Count Gismond," "Johannes Agricola in Meditation," "Porphyria's Lover," and "Soliloquy of the Spanish Cloister."

**1845** Browning's *Dramatic Romances and Lyrics* includes dramatic monologues "Pictor Ignotus," "The Bishop Orders His Tomb at Saint Praxed's Church," "The Laboratory," and "The Confessional."

**1850** Tennyson publishes *In Memoriam,* which confirms his reputation as England's leading poet. He is named Poet Laureate, successor to Wordsworth.

**1855** Tennyson's *Maud, and Other Poems* is published. "Maud" is subtitled "A Monodrama" but reads like a dramatic monologue. The work is hugely successful with the public.

Browning's *Men and Women* includes famous dramatic monologues such as "Fra Lippo Lippi," "Karshish," "Childe Roland to the Dark Tower Came," "Bishop Blougram's Apology," and "Andrea del Sarto." The work receives a lukewarm reception, like Browning's previous volumes.

**1856** William Morris writes "Riding Together," followed later by "The Judgment of God," "Concerning Geffray Teste Noire," and other dramatic monologues.

**1861** Browning returns to England from Italy after his wife's death and sets about mending his reputation.

**1862** Christina Rossetti publishes *Goblin Market and Other Poems*, which includes dramatic monologues such as "Maggie a Lady."

George Meredith publishes *Modern Love and Poems of the English Roadside*, which contains some dramatic monologues.

**1864** Tennyson's *Enoch Arden, Etc.* includes two of Tennyson's dramatic monologues in dialect, "Northern Farmer, Old Style," and "Northern Farmer, New Style."

Browning's *Dramatis Personae* includes dramatic monologues "Abt Vogler," "Rabbi Ben Ezra," and "Caliban upon Setebos." His reputation as a poet begins to improve.

**1866** Swinburne publishes *Poems and Ballads*, which contains "The Leper."

**1868** Browning publishes *The Ring and the Book*, a series of dramatic monologues.

**1871** Browning publishes *Prince Hohenstiel-Schwangau*, a lengthy dramatic monologue.

**1879** Browning's *Dramatic Idyls* includes several dramatic monologues.

**1880** Tennyson's *Ballads and Other Poems* includes dramatic monologues "Rizpah" and "In the Children's Hospital."

**1881** The Browning Society is founded in London.

**1883** Tennyson accepts a peerage from Queen Victoria and becomes Baron Tennyson.

**1885** Tennyson's *Tiresias and Other Poems* includes dramatic monologues "Tiresias" and "Despair."

**1886** Tennyson publishes *Locksley Hall Sixty Years After, Etc.*

**1893** Rudyard Kipling publishes "McAndrew's Hymn."

**1898** Thomas Hardy publishes *Wessex Poems,* which includes dramatic monologues such as "My Cicely."

**1909** Ezra Pound publishes *Personae,* which contains virtually all his dramatic monologues.

**1914** Robert Frost publishes *North of Boston* in London. The work includes "A Servant to Servants," "Home Burial," and "The Death of the Hired Man."

**1915** *North of Boston* is published in America.

Edgar Lee Masters publishes *Spoon River Anthology,* a collection of short dramatic monologues.

**1916** E.A. Robinson publishes *The Man Against the Sky,* which includes the dramatic monologue "Ben Jonson Entertains a Man from Stratford."

Frost's *Mountain Interval* includes "The Bonfire," virtually a dramatic monologue, which Frost reads at Phi Beta Kappa Day at Harvard.

Amy Lowell publishes *Men, Women and Ghosts,* which contains many dramatic monologues.

**1917** T.S. Eliot publishes *Prufrock and Other Observations,* including "The Love Song of J. Alfred Prufrock" and "Portrait of a Lady."

Louis Untermeyer publishes *These Times,* which contains some dramatic monologues.

**1919** Eliot's *Poems* includes the dramatic monologue "Gerontion."

Amy Lowell publishes *Pictures of the Floating World,* which contains some dramatic monologues.

**1920** E.A. Robinson's *The Three Taverns* includes dramatic monologues "The Three Taverns" and "John Brown."

**1921** E.A. Robinson's *Avon's Harvest* includes "Rembrandt to Rembrandt."

Langston Hughes publishes "The Negro Speaks of Rivers."

Pound advises Eliot about cuts to *The Waste Land.*

**1922** Eliot publishes *The Waste Land,* which he dedicates to Ezra Pound. The work wins the Dial Award and is to become one of the most influential poems of the twentieth century.

**1923** Louis Untermeyer publishes *Roast Leviathan,* which contains "Monolog from a Mattress."

**1924** Frost wins Pulitzer Prize for *New Hampshire,* published 1923.

**1925** Eliot publishes *The Hollow Men.*

**1932** E.A. Robinson's *Nicodemus* includes the dramatic monologue "Toussaint l'Ouverture."

**1939** Frost receives the Gold Medal for Poetry from the National Institute of Arts and Letters.

**1940** W.H. Auden publishes *Another Time,* which contains "Refugee Blues."

**1943** Frost receives his fourth Pulitzer Prize.

**1945** Pound is arrested for treason by the United States (for his broadcasts over Rome radio).

**1946** Robert Lowell publishes *Lord Weary's Castle* and wins Pulitzer Prize. The volume includes dramatic monologues "Mr. Edwards and the Spider" and "After the Surprising Conversions."

Philip Larkin writes "Wedding Wind."

**1948** Eliot is awarded the Nobel Prize and the Order of Merit.

**1949** Pound is awarded the Bollingen Prize for Poetry (for the *Pisan Cantos*).

**1951** Robert Lowell publishes *The Mills of the Kavanaughs,* which includes the dramatic monologue "Mother Marie Therese."

**1955** Randall Jarrell publishes *Selected Poems,* which includes some dramatic monologues.

**1959** U.S. Senate passes a resolution commending Frost on his eighty-fifth birthday.

**1960** Randall Jarrell's *The Woman at the Washington Zoo,* which includes the dramatic monologue of the same title, wins the National Book Award.

Ted Hughes' *Lupercal* includes "Hawk Roosting."

**1961** Frost reads "The Gift Outright" at President Kennedy's inauguration.

**1963** Frost is awarded the Bollingen Prize for Poetry.

**1965** Randall Jarrell's *The Lost World* includes dramatic monologues "Next Day" and "The Lost Children."

**1968** Zbigniew Herbert publishes *Selected Poems* in English, which includes some dramatic monologues (translated from the Polish by Czeslaw Milosz and Peter Dale Scott).

**1969** Richard Howard's *Untitled Subjects,* which includes many dramatic monologues, wins Pulitzer Prize for 1970.

**1971** Richard Howard publishes *Findings,* which includes a dramatic monologue spoken by Browning.

**1977** Allen Tate publishes his *Collected Poems 1919–1976,* containing several dramatic monologues.

**1980** Czeslaw Milosz wins the Nobel Prize for literature.

**1984** Richard Howard's *Lining Up* contains a section ("Homage to Nadar") that includes several dramatic monologues addressed to various French artists, musicians, and men of letters.

**1985** Zbigniew Herbert publishes *Report from the Besieged City,* which includes some dramatic monologues (translated from the Polish by John Carpenter and Bogdana Carpenter).

**1988** Czeslaw Milosz publishes his *Collected Poems 1931–1987*, containing translations of some of his work in Polish, including several dramatic monologues.

**1994** Richard Howard's *Like Most Revelations* includes some dramatic monologues.

# Chapter 1

# OVERVIEW

## Definitions and Characteristic Features

The dramatic monologue is a type of poem composed, as the name "monologue" implies, in the first person. Yet thousands of first-person lyrics are not dramatic monologues; any definition of the latter depends therefore to a large extent on distinguishing it from purely lyric poems. We are concerned in this section with exploring this distinction as well as with other features of the dramatic monologue, including the various implications of the word "dramatic."

As an illustration of the genre let us look briefly at an extract from "My Last Duchess," one of the most famous of dramatic monologues, by its most renowned practitioner, Robert Browning:

> That's my last Duchess painted on the wall,
> Looking as if she were alive . . .

```
.............................. She had
```
A heart—how shall I say?—too soon made glad,
Too easily impressed; she liked whate'er
She looked on, and her looks went everywhere.
Sir, 'twas all one! My favour at her breast,
The dropping of the daylight in the West,
The bough of cherries some officious fool
Broke in the orchard for her, the white mule
She rode with round the terrace—all and each
Would draw from her alike the approving speech,
Or blush, at least. She thanked men,—good! but thanked
Somehow—I know not how—as if she ranked
My gift of a nine-hundred-years-old name
With anybody's gift . . .

. . . . . . . . . . . . . . .
. . . Oh sir, she smiled, no doubt,
Whene'er I passed her; but who passed without
Much the same smile? This grew; I gave commands;
Then all smiles stopped together. There she stands
As if alive. Will't please you rise? We'll meet
The company below, then. I repeat,
The Count your master's known munificence
Is ample warrant that no just pretence
Of mine for dowry will be disallowed;
Though his fair daughter's self, as I avowed
At starting, is my object. Nay, we'll go
Together down, sir. Notice Neptune, though,
Taming a sea-horse, thought a rarity,
Which Claus of Innsbruck cast in bronze for me!

Note that the "I" who speaks this poem is the Duke (of Ferrara),
husband to the late Duchess of the title. He is talking to an interlocutor, a Count's envoy; and his speech, if not exactly colloquial,
at least displays some features of oral discourse such as ellipsis
("Will't"), hesitations or disclaimers ("I know not how," "how
shall I say?"), interjections ("Oh sir," "good!"). The reader
receives a powerful impression of the Duke's personality, including aspects of it that the Duke is perhaps unaware of revealing or
indeed of possessing, such as cruelty ("Then all smiles stopped
together"), excessive pride in his "nine-hundred-years-old
name," and self-satisfaction ("Which Claus of Innsbruck cast in
bronze for me!").

## Definitions of the dramatic monologue

Attempts to define the dramatic monologue in recent years have tended to stumble over two contradictory hurdles: that of being too restrictive or, on the contrary, too loose. Early critics were tempted to define the dramatic monologue by cataloging various features said to be essential to the genre, including colloquial language or at least language with an oral flavor; the presence of an auditor; psychological self-revelation on the part of the speaker, as well as clear identification of the speaker in a well-defined spatial and temporal context.[1] Although many of Browning's most famous monologues, including "My Last Duchess," meet these criteria, many others fail to satisfy them all simultaneously. Similarly, when we turn to other authors of poems generally accepted as dramatic monologues, we find that Tennyson does not use oral discourse, as a glance at "Ulysses" or "Tithonus" amply demonstrates, and that his and Ezra Pound's dramatic monologues rely much less than Browning's on psychological self-revelation. Furthermore, Pound's monologues, such as "Cino" and "Marvoil," do not presuppose the presence of an auditor, nor does Tennyson's "Locksley Hall" after the first stanza, or T.S. Eliot's "Love Song of J. Alfred Prufrock" if the phrase "you and I" of the first line is taken, as it generally is, to mean two halves of the self.

Apparently, therefore, criteria such as oral discourse, presence of an auditor, and psychological self-revelation, though commonly found in Browning's most successful poems, are not essential to the dramatic monologue. Only one feature is common to all the poems mentioned above, namely their identification of the speaker as someone other than the poet, whether a mythical figure like Ulysses and Tithonus, a historical one like Marvoil, or a fictional speaker such as Prufrock or the soldier of "Locksley Hall."

A definition that adequately describes only Browning's dramatic monologues (and not all of those) is clearly unsatisfactory as a generic term. Robert Langbaum, in his influential and valuable book, *The Poetry of Experience*, abandoned the attempt to define the dramatic monologue by a list of characteristics in favor of an analysis of its "*way* of meaning," which he sees as predicated upon the reader's sympathy with the poem's speaker and his experience.[2] This guideline, too, is controversial: first, many readers feel very little sympathy with some of Browning's protagonists, such as the Bishop of Saint Praxed's Church, the Duke in "My Last Duchess," or the speaker of "Soliloquy of the Spanish Cloister"; second, a tendency to sympathize with a first-person speaker is characteristic of any genre, not of the dramatic monologue alone.

Many later critics have defined the dramatic monologue in much looser terms or avoided definition altogether. Thus Frances Carleton asserts that "the dramatic monologue . . . defies a firm definition," and Roma King that "Browning's short poems . . . defy rigid classification." Donald Hair's "combination of the drama and the lyric" is true enough but unhelpful, since many lyric poems contain an element of drama without being dramatic monologues. Park Honan says of his own loose definition that it "implies that many poems might be considered as both lyrics *and* dramatic monologues" and that this view "seems to reflect a truth."[3] Yet it appears imperative to distinguish between dramatic monologue and lyric poem, since the latter category is massive and would swamp the dramatic monologue completely. Besides, most poetry-lovers would agree that reading a dramatic monologue is a different experience from reading a lyric poem.

### Distinction between dramatic monologue and lyric

The confusion between the two arises because both are written in the first person. Yet there is a difference between the "I" of the dramatic monologue and that of the lyric. Consider the voice speaking in "My Last Duchess," quoted above, or in "Andrea del Sarto": "But do not let us quarrel any more, / No, my Lucrezia; bear with me for once"; in "Cino" by Ezra Pound: "Bah! I have sung women in three cities, / But it is all the same; / And I will sing of the sun"; or in Tennyson's "Ulysses": "It little profits that an idle king, / By this still hearth, among these barren crags, / Match'd with an aged wife, I mete and dole / Unequal laws unto a savage race"; or in Eliot's "Love Song of J. Alfred Prufrock": "Let us go then, you and I . . . ." The speakers of these poems are fictional, mythical, or historical characters, clearly identified in these instances by their names in the poems' titles or subtitles. In other dramatic monologues the protagonists may not be named but nevertheless are identified by vari-

4

ous means such as social title (Duke, Bishop, and so on); profession, as in William Blake's "The Chimney Sweeper" or Tennyson's "Northern Farmer" poems; or by the possession of some other distinguishing feature (Blake's "The Little Black Boy" or "The Leper" by Swinburne).

## Objectivity

The reader of poems such as these perceives their speakers as Other, as separate identities. The poems are "dramatic" in the sense Browning meant when he described his *Dramatic Lyrics,* in the Advertisement to the first edition of 1842, as being "though for the most part Lyric in expression, always Dramatic in principle, and so many utterances of so many imaginary persons, not mine." In other words, by "Dramatic" he means "objective": the speaker of the poem is not the poet himself.

Let us turn now to the "I" of poems not normally thought of as dramatic monologues, and consider who is the speaker, for example, in Wordsworth's "Daffodils":

> I wander'd lonely as a cloud
> That floats on high o'er vales and hills,
> When all at once I saw a crowd,
> A host, of golden daffodils;
> Beside the lake, beneath the trees,
> Fluttering and dancing in the breeze.

Who says "I" in this poem? The student is tempted to reply "Wordsworth," since he is the author of the poem; but it is dangerous to equate the lyric "I" with the poet's biographical "I." We cannot be sure that Wordsworth himself took that walk and saw that host of daffodils. There is nothing to prevent a poet from conflating events, sensations, or impressions that he experienced on different occasions, from displacing them, or indeed from inventing them altogether. Sometimes, as in the case of Lamartine's "Le Lac," for example, we know enough about a poet's life to be fairly sure he is describing his own experience; yet we may still have reservations: did Mme Charles really say the words attributed to her in the poem? Certainly not in verse! Occasionally a poet will deliberately indicate that he is writing about himself, by the title, as Byron's "On This Day I Complete

5

My Thirty-Sixth Year" or the long title of Wordsworth's "Tintern Abbey" ("Lines Composed a Few Miles Above Tintern Abbey On Revisiting the Banks of the Wye During a Tour. July 13, 1798"). Wordsworth himself, however, confesses that his "Lines Written While Sailing in a Boat at Evening" were not, in fact, written in a boat; the "I" of this poem, of "Daffodils," and of most lyrics is what Ekbert Faas calls a "self-dramatization"— a projection of his own self, supplied by the poet, a poetic *persona* that may, or may not, come close to being his biographical self.[4]

This view of the lyric "I" as a persona led many New Critics to consider all poetry as dramatic in this sense. Reuben Brower affirms that "a poem is a dramatic fiction no less than a play," and John Crowe Ransom claims that "all poetry . . . maintains certain dramatic features. The poet does not speak in his own but in an assumed character . . . in an assumed situation." He goes so far as to assert that any poem "may be said to be a dramatic monologue" and that Browning "only literalized . . . the thing that had always been the poem's lawful form."[5] Is Wordsworth's "Daffodils" therefore a dramatic monologue? Surely not; for although the "I" of such a lyric does not necessarily, or not absolutely, represent the poet himself, it also does not represent anyone else, either—unlike the "I" of "My Last Duchess" or "Ulysses" or other dramatic monologues. A characteristic feature of the lyric "I" is precisely this vagueness that allows the reader to equate it with the poet, perhaps; to identify with it himself, or herself; or to see it as a universal "I" belonging to no one and to everyone. Thus the lyric, as Sharon Cameron suggests, "is a departure . . . from the finite constrictions of identity," positing a speaker whose "origin remains deliberately unspecified."[6] The "I" who "wander'd lonely as a cloud" can refer to Wordsworth, or to any reader or reciter of the poem.

Such is not the case with the "I" of a dramatic monologue. When Ulysses complains that "Match'd with an aged wife, I mete and dole / Unequal laws unto a savage race," we understand these as his words, uttered in his specific situation. We hear the speech of a dramatic monologue as belonging to and characteristic of its speaker. As William Rogers says of dramatic monologues "we feel the 'otherness' of the speaker's voice as a difference not only from the author, but from ourselves."[7]

## Distance

Thus dramatic monologues assume a certain separation or *distance* between poet and speaker on the one hand and between reader and speaker on the other. The speaker's "otherness" can be established by a name, title, or profession; by dates; by the creation of an atmosphere characteristic of a particular place or era, be it the 16th-century Italy of Andrea del Sarto, the mythical Greece of Ulysses, or the 20th-century drawing-room of J. Alfred Prufrock. Such details serve to place the protagonist in a spatial or temporal context that helps to identify him, for example, as the dying Bishop of Saint Praxed's Church, as a monk in a Spanish cloister, or as the lonely 20th-century lady of Eliot's "Portrait of a Lady," with her lilac, her Chopin, and her tea. The poet may also create a "moral distance" between speaker and reader by presenting reprehensible personae—a technique often adopted by Browning; or he may establish historical distance, by using a figure from history or myth, as speaker. A somewhat different means of distancing the speaker is through the use of irony—a distinctive feature of Eliot's dramatic monologues.

## Marginal cases

We may assert, then, despite Ransom's claim, that not all poems are dramatic monologues. The reader of a lyric poem may identify closely with its speaker, who is not necessarily particularized or identified in any way; whereas the "I" of a dramatic monologue is experienced as separate from both poet and reader, as "other." However, the reader's perception of the speaker's autonomy may be uncertain if the latter is, deliberately or otherwise, insufficiently particularized. Ultimately, in cases where the speaker of a poem is identified only in very vague terms, the reader may or may not experience the poem as a dramatic monologue, depending on his perception of the protagonist's identity. Thus, the speaker of Browning's "Porphyria's Lover," though not named himself, is clearly identifiable as Other by his designation as the lover of Porphyria. However, the reader of a monologue entitled simply "The Lover," unless the speaker becomes more closely identified, might view the poem simply as a lyric whose "I" could refer to the poet or be adopted by the reader for himself. Such an instance is Mörike's "Lied eines Verliebten," cited by Käte Hamburger, in which, as she says, "the title's vague reference to 'a man in love' can be a more or less transparent camouflage for the empirical I of the poet."[8] It is largely a question of degree: the greater the distance implied, by various means, between poet and speaker on the one hand and speaker and reader on the other, the more likely we are to assess the poem as a dramatic monologue; when the distance is only slight, or uncertain, we might view the poem as a lyric and perhaps identify with the speaker.

## The double voice of the dramatic monologue

Marginal cases such as these do not invalidate a distinction between dramatic monologue and lyric poem based on identification of the speaker. He/she may be more or less thoroughly characterized, placed in a more or less specific context; but if we know the Duke of Ferrara is speaking, then we accept that the words of the poem are his; . . . although this may not be completely true. For as we listen to the Duke telling us his story as he sees it, we cannot remain unaware of the poet's presence in the poem, shaping a somewhat different version of the story. The most characteristic feature of the speech of a dramatic monologue results from this inherent dichotomy between the voice of the poem's speaker and that of the poet, who is inevitably present. The Duke is plainly very aware of the dignity of his own status, proud of his nine-hundred-years-old name, and accepts as his rightful due the artistic tributes of Fra Pandolf and Claus of Innsbruck. His attitude to his wife is that she deserved punishment for her loose ways, and that he was justified in punishing her. Nevertheless the reader receives a different impression: of a hard-hearted, arrogant, and self-satisfied man who has probably taken a criminal vengeance on his charming and innocent wife. The dramatic irony inherent in this "disequilibrium with what the speaker reveals and understands" about himself (Langbaum, 146) is typical not only of "My Last Duchess" but of "The Bishop Orders His Tomb," "The Laboratory," "Porphyria's Lover," "Andrea del Sarto," "Karshish," and "Cleon," to name but a few of the most well-known poems from Browning's *Dramatic Lyrics, Dramatic Romances,* and *Men and Women.*

The split resulting from the fact that the poem's words are simultaneously those of an identified individual and of the poet represents a distinctive characteristic of the dramatic monologue in general and one of its most interesting features. Rogers sees this linguistic anomaly as a way of distinguishing between lyric poems and dramatic monologues (which he calls "lyrics of anomalous voice"):

> Thus, the *essential* difference between lyrics of anomalous voice and other lyrics is that our interpretations of the former call particular attention to the "doubleness" of voice. In interpreting a poem like "Tintern Abbey" we say that there is no difference, or almost none, between author and speaker . . . . With lyrics of anomalous voice, however, the "doubleness" of author and speaker, potentially part of every poem, is made the point of the poem as interpreted. (Rogers, 81)

Loy D. Martin, too, argues that "discursive splitting . . . helps us to recognize dramatic monologues"; and Ralph Rader comments that the very fact of a dramatic monologue's being written in verse makes the reader aware of the inherent duality of the poem's language. Referring to "My Last Duchess" Rader says:

> If we ask ourselves whether in reading the poem we imaginatively hear the words of the poem as spoken by the Duke, we discover of course that we do. If we then ask if we hear the rhymes in the poem as part of the Duke's speech, we discover that we do not. This small but potent fact suggests even without further analysis that the poet's presence in the poem is a fundamental aspect of its form.

Martin, agreeing with this assessment, adds that, in the dramatic monologue, language "seems to operate both at a level that is consciously 'poetic' in some traditional sense and at a separate syntactic, semantic, or merely 'message' level." And Alan Sinfield affirms that we "experience the 'I' of the poem as a character in his own right but at the same time sense the author's voice through him." [9]

This phenomenon, of hearing two distinct voices in a single speech act, is referred to by Mikhail Bakhtin as dialogism, and is a concept that has proved fruitful in the study of narrative discourse. Double-voiced discourse, he says, "serves two speakers at the same time and expresses simultaneously two different intentions: the direct intention of the character who is speaking, and the refracted intention of the author": a perfect description of the dramatic monologue, though Bakhtin is referring here to novel-istic discourse. He gives examples from Pushkin, Dickens, and Dostoevsky. Poetry, however, according to Bakhtin, is monologi-cal: it is "illumined by one unitary and indisputable discourse." Clearly, Bakhtin is referring to lyric poetry, as a footnote seems to indicate ("It goes without saying that we continually advance as typical the extreme to which poetic genres aspire"); and in such poetry the "language of the poet is *his* language" and his alone. "Each word must express the poet's *meaning* directly and without mediation; there must be no distance between the poet and his word."[10] Although these words may well apply to the lyric, we have seen that in the dramatic monologue, on the contrary, the notion of distance is crucial. Bakhtin's statements relate the lan-guage of the dramatic monologue to that of the novel, and indeed the dramatic monologue has other novelistic qualities that tend, again, to distinguish it from the lyric poem.

### Novelistic qualities of the dramatic monologue

One feature that relates the dramatic monologue to the novel—and differentiates it from the lyric—is its characteristic narrative element. Like the protagonists of a novel, Browning's personae have a past, and as in a novel we attend to the gradual unfolding of their story (for example, in "Andrea del Sarto," "The Bishop Orders His Tomb," and "Fra Lippo Lippi"), or of a particularly significant incident in their lives. The stories may be less elabo-rate in dramatic monologues by other poets, such as Tennyson and Pound, but a certain narrative element is always present, which is not true, say, of Keats' "Ode to Autumn." Jonathan Culler distinguishes between "two forces in poetry, the narrative and the apostrophic," and concludes that "the lyric is characteris-tically the triumph of the apostrophic," for "Nothing need hap-pen in an apostrophic poem, as the great Romantic odes amply demonstrate."[11]

A realistic setting, in both time and space, is another aspect of the novel that is often found also in dramatic monologues. The "first task" of characters in narratives, comments Sharon Cameron, "is to particularize themselves"; whereas the origins of lyric speak-ers remain "deliberately unspecified" and they move in a world of "temporal indeterminacy" (Cameron, 208, 247). Some poets go to greater lengths than others in particularizing speakers; Browning especially likes to pinpoint his personae in space and time and give them a realistic name and a social occupation or status. Thus we have an Evelyn Hope, a Count Gismond, a Bishop Blougram; we hear monks and bishops, soldiers, painters; wives, lovers; dukes, counts, fashionable ladies. Tennyson, in contrast, is apt to choose mythical protagonists, the circumstances of whose existence are less well defined. Both Browning and Pound frequently take characters from history, which automatically guarantees their objective, "real" existence as autonomous entities, independent of their creator and of the reader; and they give their speakers specific personality traits that they reveal in everything they say and sometimes in their very manner of speaking.

Although the Duke of Ferrara speaks in rhymed couplets, the syntactic line rarely corresponds to the verse line, so that the "poetic" level of language is played down and the impression conveyed is almost one of natural speech:

> That's my last Duchess painted on the wall,
> Looking as if she were alive. I call
> That piece a wonder, now: Frà Pandolf's hands
> Worked busily a day, and there she stands.

The effect of natural speech can be achieved not only by rhythm, of course, but also by the use of repetitions, interruptions, relatively simple syntactic structures and vocabulary, and interjections such as Marvoil's "Me! in this damn'd inn of Avignon," in Pound's "Marvoil"; or Fra Lippo Lippi's "Zooks, who's to blame?" or the famous "Gr-r-r-" at the beginning of "Soliloquy of the Spanish Cloister." Such elements are analyzed in the commentaries on individual poems; meanwhile, here is an example of the opposite trend, Tennyson's Ulysses addressing his mariners:

> Much have I seen and known,—cities of men
> And manners, climates, councils, governments,
> Myself not least, but honor'd of them all,—
> And drunk delight of battle with my peers,
> Far on the ringing plains of windy Troy.
> I am a part of all that I have met;
> Yet all experience is an arch wherethro'
> Gleams that untravell'd world whose margin fades
> For ever and for ever when I move.

11

Clearly, not all dramatic monologues attempt to imitate oral speech. Like the dialogue of stage drama, the dramatic monologue may imitate, as far as possible, the flavor of spoken language, or it may forgo any such pretension to oral realism. Noting the existence of lyrical dramatic monologues such as those of Tennyson, Sinfield compares them with stage drama: just as the latter does not have to be realistic or naturalistic, but can be lyrical, so we can expect to find more, or less, lyrical types of dramatic monologue. He concludes that poems like "Tithonus," Eliot's "A Song for Simeon," and Pound's "La Fraisne" "are varieties of dramatic monologue, not some other genre" (Sinfield, 20).

The more realistic detail the poet supplies, the more the reader tends, paradoxically, to regard the poem as he would a fiction, a semblance of life, because the procedure of naming characters and fitting them into a situation, a time and a place is typically novelistic and mimetic. Thus we find critics asserting—disparagingly—that "it is as novels . . . that many of Browning's poems offer themselves," or that Browning is a "novelist in verse."[12] This assertion results from the very nature of the dramatic monologue, which lies between lyric poetry and fiction, being a poem spoken by a fictional persona, or by a fictionalized historical or mythological persona. Käte Hamburger refers to this feature as a "feint," in her analysis of the "role-poem" (*Rollengedicht*), which Sinfield summarizes thus: "Dramatic monologue feigns because it pretends to be something other than what it is: an invented speaker masquerades in the first person which customarily signifies the poet's voice" (Sinfield, 25). Hamburger sees "fictionality" as the main point of difference between lyric poetry and narrative prose or drama, and considers that the dramatic monologue lies somewhere between these two genres, having the "logical structure" of fiction while being written in the first person like lyric (Hamburger, 292).[13] Browning seems almost to anticipate this view when he declares in his Advertisement that his *Dramatic Lyrics* are "though for the most part Lyric in expression, always Dramatic in principle." The author of the *Dramatic Lyrics*, *Dramatic Romances*, *Dramatis Personae*, and *Dramatic Idylls* never used the term "dramatic monologue"; however, his insistence on the word in his titles is remarkable. And though by "dramatic" he means, as we have seen, "objective" rather than "full of conflict, of drama," his poems certainly are dramatic in this last sense also. They present "exciting," tense situations, such as Fra Lippo Lippi's arrest, Porphyria's murder, and the Bishop's imminent death. The events implied in "The Laboratory," "Porphyria's Lover," or "My Last Duchess" could form the plots of fictional stories or historical dramas.

### The dramatic element

Drama involves conflict and tension. For example, in many of Browning's dramatic monologues a certain tension arises, as in "My Last Duchess," from the discrepancy between the speaker's assessment of his situation and the reader's understanding of it. In these poems a conflict often is apparent also between the speaker and the world around him, as between the Bishop ordering his tomb and his nephews, the speaker in the Spanish cloister and Brother Lawrence, or Fra Lippo Lippi and society in general. The immediate source of tension in Fra Lippo's situation is his apprehension by the night patrol, but it becomes evident that his nature and lifestyle also bring him into conflict with the morality of his society, which in turn has repercussions for his art.

There is no internal conflict, or development, within these characters, who, like the Duke of Ferrara, strive to justify their own viewpoint to others. In some monologues, however, the speaker is in conflict not with the external world but with himself. Ulysses is engaged in an internal debate with himself about whether to leave Ithaca or stay; the speaker of "Locksley Hall" comes to grips with his own painful memories; inner division and conflict is implied by the very form of Prufrock's "Let us go then, you and I." Here the interlocutor addressed as "you" is the other half of the speaker's own self, since "The Love Song of J. Alfred Prufrock" is a soliloquy. Very often, however, dramatic monologues constitute, in fact, one side of a dialogue, so that any speech in the second person is directed at an interlocutor. The introduction of second-person address tends to enhance the dramatic effect of the poem, dialogue being the distinctive form of stage drama. Browning attempts to give the flavor of it in his monologues by inserting remarks either directly addressed to a silent auditor or patently prompted by an implied comment or gesture on his part. Thus Andrea del Sarto addresses Lucrezia when she evidently loses the thread of his story:

> Still, all I care for, if he spoke the truth,
> (What he? why who but Michel Angelo?
> Do you forget already words like those?) . . . .

The Duke of Ferrara reacts to a self-effacing gesture of his interlocutor when he says "Nay, we'll go / Together down, sir," and the Bishop of Saint Praxed's is quick to notice the hesitancy of the reluctant Anselm:

> Draw round my bed: Is Anselm keeping back?
>
> . . . . . . . . . . . What do they whisper thee,
> Child of my bowels, Anselm?

Some critics maintain that the presence of an auditor is essential in a dramatic monologue. Thus Martin claims that all dramatic monologues "at least fantasize a listener, and this is chiefly what differentiates them from lyrics or extracted soliloquies" (Martin, 133); but in soliloquies that are not "extracted," such as "Prufrock," the speaker may also fantasize a listener, even if it is himself. To insist that a dramatic monologue must have an auditor would exclude not only "Prufrock," but Pound's monologues, Tennyson's "Locksley Hall" and "Maud," and several of Browning's poems, including "Porphyria's Lover," "Johannes Agricola in Meditation," and "Soliloquy of the Spanish Cloister." There seems no reason why a dramatic monologue should not be a soliloquy; in such poems the conflict tends to be more internal, but they are not necessarily less dramatic for that.

Certainly the speaker of a dramatic monologue is involved in a drama of some kind, so that both meanings of the word "dramatic" are relevant to the definition of the genre, that is, Browning's sense of "objective" as well as the suggestion of tension or conflict. Thus a purely narrative poem in the first person, such as Browning's "The Flight of the Duchess," does not read as a dramatic monologue: there is drama in the poem, but the speaker is not involved in it; he simply narrates it.

## Character portrayal

In an attempt to differentiate between dramatic monologue and lyric, Ralph Rader posits a third category, the "mask lyric," whose persona, rather than being a "simulated natural person," that is, a character like those we usually expect to find in novels or drama, merely represents an "aspect of [the poet's] own subjective situation." Poems such as "Ulysses," "Childe Roland to the Dark Tower Came," and "The Love Song of J. Alfred Prufrock" are, according to Rader, "really a kind of indirect lyric" spoken by an "artificial person projected from the poet."[14] How can one tell, however, from reading the poem, that Prufrock is not speaking as an autonomous creation but expresses an aspect of Eliot's own "subjective situation"? Besides, we have seen that speakers of dramatic monologues are not totally autonomous: we always hear the poet's voice through theirs. Rader's distinction ignores, too, the dramatic element, present in "Ulysses," "Prufrock," and "Childe Roland," that the term "mask lyric" tends to play down. If poems such as "Prufrock," "Childe Roland," and "Ulysses"—and presumably other monologues by Tennyson—cannot be called dramatic monologues, the value of the term as a generic category is curtailed severely, being applicable only to certain of Browning's poems. It is true that "Childe Roland," "Prufrock," and "Ulysses" place less emphasis than many dramatic monologues on character portrayal, but the speakers are named and identified and therefore perceived by the reader as other than the poet. Rather than being "projected from the poet," I would suggest that these personae illustrate aspects of universal human experience. Prufrock represents a certain type of modern man; Ulysses faces a common human dilemma: the choice between doing what social and family obligations require of him, namely to stay at home and rule as king over Ithaca, or doing what he profoundly believes he needs to do in order to be himself, that is, set off again on his nautical travels. Childe Roland, too, sets off on an adventure only to find, in the words of E. Warwick Slinn, that in "seeking in the tower an external object as the goal of experience, [he] discovers instead the self as a subject which is the centre of experience."[15]

The adoption of a universal, often mythical, figure as speaker precludes the detailed contexts provided in most of Browning's monologues, hence, the "irreal, fluid and symbolic scene" that Rader associates with the "mask lyric" (Rader 1984, 106). There is also less emphasis on character portrayal in poems with such speakers: a universal or mythical figure does not display specific traits of personality, does not usually have a "character."

In most of Browning's famous dramatic monologues, in contrast, the portrayal of character is so central that many critics have seen that as his intrinsic aim.[16] In poems such as "My Last Duchess," "Soliloquy of the Spanish Cloister," "Porphyria's Lover," "Fra Lippo Lippi," "The Bishop Orders His Tomb at Saint Praxed's Church," and "Andrea del Sarto," Browning's world resembles, once again, that of realist fiction in that it constitutes a "mimesis" or imitation of reality, presenting well-defined characters intended to simulate real human beings and recognizable as individuals distinct from the author. Characters like the Duke of Ferrara, the Bishop of Saint Praxed's, and Fra Lippo Lippi are so well delineated that we have the feeling of knowing them, of being able to predict, for example, how they would react in other, hypothetical, circumstances beyond the scope of the poem. Through their speech and their actions we assess their character, which is how we know most people in real life. To this extent they appear to be "whole" characters with identifiable, stable personalities. Herbert F. Tucker asserts that "Browning certainly believed in the self,"[17] and Ekbert Faas implies that Browning's "sense of the self as 'centre of all things'" (*Pauline*, l. 274) is "outdated" (Faas, 70). The kind of self Browning envisages here in *Pauline* is, however, a very abstract notion that expressly belies the concept of personality or character:

> I am made up of an intensest life,
> Of a most clear idea of consciousness
> Of self, distinct from all its qualities,
> From all affections, passions, feelings, powers.
> (*Pauline*, ll. 268–71)

A "consciousness . . . distinct from all its qualities" is hardly a character, but simply an awareness of being; the "qualities" themselves may change. We are accustomed nowadays to thinking of personality as indeterminate and as varying according to circumstances and social roles. Slinn, in his book with the significant title *Browning and the Fictions of Identity,* adds that the older concept, of selfhood as a stable entity, "can already be seen dissolving with Browning" (Slinn, 16). For in fact Browning's dramatic monologues question the nature of personality and the possibility of its adequate expression. Thanks to the double voice of the dramatic monologue, the reader of "My Last Duchess" gains a different impression of the Duke's real nature from the image he has of himself. The same duality affects our view of the Bishop at Saint Praxed's, Porphyria's lover, the speaker of the "Soliloquy," and Andrea del Sarto. As Slinn suggests, "Browning questions the truth of experience by exposing . . . the fallibility of his speakers" (Slinn, ix). One's sense of self relies on the recognition of others, as Lee Erikson points out: "For Browning, the dramatic monologue is ultimately not the expression of a stable, autonomous self but the drama of a speaker's search for the recognition of others that will give the speaker his or her sense of self."[18] Browning's monologues raise the question of how well we can really know others and ourselves, and of how it is possible, if at all, to express this self in words. Doubts about the possibility of portraying an "I" that represents a whole, stable subject were linked for Browning with the problem of language, which cannot express "wholes" but can merely present "the whole / By parts, the simultaneous and the sole / By the successive and the many" (*Sordello*, Book II, ll. 593–95). Clyde de L. Ryals summarizes as follows the difficulties inherent in trying to speak the truth about oneself: "1) language is inadequate to express it; 2) one's point of view . . . permits only certain perspectives on truth; and 3) one's sense of self, one's *amour propre*, necessitates special pleading."[19]

In general, the dramatic monologue "is a form which almost invariably raises questions about personality . . . so that dramatic tension becomes focused on conflicts about self-conception" (Slinn, ix). The importance of these issues of personality and self-expression was no doubt relevant to the sudden flowering of the dramatic monologue in the mid-19th century; but before analyzing the reasons for that phenomenon, we should look at earlier origins of the dramatic monologue in previous centuries.

## Origins and Development of the Dramatic Monologue

The term "dramatic monologue" was first used in 1857, according to A. Dwight Culler, and first applied to Browning's poetry in 1859.[20] Though the form existed namelessly, or with other names, before the 19th century, and though many 20th-century examples can be found, it certainly blossomed in England in the mid-

19th century. In this section we examine circumstances of time and place: why did the dramatic monologue flourish in the 19th century, why in England, and to what extent does it exist in other national literatures?

### Early examples of the dramatic monologue

Precursors to the dramatic monologue can be found in abundance both in early English literature and in classical literature. Benjamin Fuson cites Ovid's *Heroides*, poems representing letters of famous women to famous men, for example, Dido to Aeneas, Penelope to Ulysses (Fuson, 23). This epistolary form of monologue was imitated by many English poets before the 19th century, such as Samuel Daniel, whose "Letter from Octavia to Marcus Antonius" dates from 1599; Michael Drayton, who wrote a series of letter-poems entitled *England's Heroicall Epistles* (1619); and Alexander Pope, whose "Eloisa to Abelard" (1717) provides the most satisfying example of this type of dramatic monologue before the 19th century.

A common linguistic exercise used in education, called *prosopopoeia*, involved writing and/or declaiming poems with identified speakers. Prosopopoeia was considered a useful study because it required the writer to establish and illustrate the speaker's identity, profession, social rank, character, and speech habits; it had been recommended by Quintilian (*Institutio Oratoria*, III, viii, 49–54). The prosopopoeia illustrated one of Plato's comments on poetic voice, namely that when a poet like Homer presents the speech of a character, he "makes his own style as much like that of the indicated speaker as possible."[21]

One of the most common types of poem written in an assumed voice was the complaint—composed, as its name implies, to express sadness or grief occasioned, usually, by death or by love. Such poems often were written in the first voice, that of the poet speaking in his own person—but this did not imply, as it might for a Romantic poet, that the grief was his own, genuine and sincere. The complaint, like other poetic forms from classical times until the 18th century, was a conventional mode; poets assumed the voice and persona belonging to a given form without necessarily committing themselves to a sincere expression of their own personal emotions. Robert C. Elliott's comment regarding Classical poets remained true until the beginnings of Romanticism: "For them sincerity is a function of style, involving a relation between the artist and the public; it has to do with the presentation of a self appropriate to the kind of verse being written, to the genre, not with the personality of the poet" (Elliott, 43).

However, the complaint was also composed, very often, in the voice that Plato refers to as "imitation," since it imitates the speech of a specific, identified speaker; such instances may be considered precursors of the dramatic monologue. To be sure, one would not necessarily consider all of them to be full-fledged dramatic monologues, because the speakers are often identified only very vaguely, for example, as "a shepherd," and the dramatic element may also be lacking. Nevertheless, the potential clearly is there. During the Renaissance most English poets wrote complaints, based on a classical model developed by Theocritus and other Greek poets as well as by Virgil. Shakespeare has a "Lover's Complaint"; Milton's "Lycidas" belongs in this category; and Andrew Marvell wrote a series of mowers' complaints (published posthumously in 1681). "Damon the Mower" begins with three stanzas in the third person introducing the love-sick Damon, and ends with two stanzas describing his reaction when he injures himself with his own scythe; but the rest of the poem reads like a dramatic monologue spoken in the first person by Damon. Another poem, "The Mower's Song," is written entirely in the mower's own words:

> My mind was once the true survey
> Of all these meadows fresh and gay,
> And in the greenness of the grass
> Did see its hopes as in a glass;
> When Juliana came, and she
> What I do to the grass, does to my thoughts and me.

Use of the first person—whether in poetry or prose—encourages the reader to sympathize with the speaker, so that it is particularly appropriate not only for love poems but for poems whose speakers are unjustly treated or otherwise unfortunate. Thus we find Joseph Warton's "The Dying Indian," from the 1740s, in which the Indian, who has been struck by a poisoned arrow, bemoans some of the injustices done to his race:

> .................... —O my son,
> I feel the venom busy in my breast,
> Approach, and bring my crown, deck'd with the teeth
> Of that bold Christian who first dar'd deflow'r
> The virgins of the sun; and, dire to tell!
> Robb'd Pachacamac's altar of its gems!

Later in the 18th century come "The Negro's Complaint" by William Cowper (1788), Wordsworth's "Complaint of a Forsaken Indian Woman" (1798), Robert Burns's "Holy Willie's Prayer" (1799), William Blake's "The Chimney Sweeper" (1789), and "The Little Black Boy," also by Blake:

> My mother bore me in the southern wild,
> And I am black, but O, my soul is white!
> White as an angel is the English child,
> But I am black, as if bereaved of light.

Fuson claims to have discovered hundreds of dramatic monologues written before the Victorian era, including the Anglo-Saxon "Banished Wife's Lament"; Chaucer's "Wife of Bath's Tale," which though part of a longer poem in fact, displays many features typical of dramatic monologues, such as character-revelation, oral speech, and the presence of auditors; John Skelton's "Boke of Philip Sparowe" (a girl's lament for her dead bird); as well as poems by Joseph Warton, Cowper, Gray, Blake, Burns, Wordsworth, and others (Fuson, 9–10; 22, n. 29).

During the early 19th century, the major Romantic poets were concerned principally with lyric poetry and were not particularly attracted to the dramatic monologue. Byron's "Prisoner of Chillon" (1816) is, however, a dramatic monologue, spoken by the prisoner, the 16th-century Geneva patriot Bonnivard:

> My hair is gray, but not with years,
> Nor grew it white
> In a single night,
> As men's have grown from sudden fears.

Byron's "Lament of Tasso" is also a dramatic monologue, like Shelley's "The Indian Serenade" (1822); Walter Savage Landor's "Corinna, from Athens, to Tanagra" or "The Maid's Lament"; and Wordsworth's "The Affliction of Margaret" (1807), in which a mother laments that she has had no news of her son for seven years. Meanwhile, a host of minor poets, such as Robert Southey, John Clare, Leigh Hunt, Walter Savage Landor, and Thomas Hood, were writing dramatic monologues, some highly sentimental, some melodramatic, some lacking in drama. As Fuson points out, the genre existed in the early 19th century, though lacking a name, but it remained to Browning and Tennyson to exploit its psychological possibilities (Fuson, 74–75).

## The flowering of the dramatic monologue in the 19th century

Certainly the most famous practitioners of the dramatic monologue are Tennyson and Browning, who began to compose such poems almost simultaneously but independently of each other. The year 1842 saw the publication of Browning's *Dramatic Lyrics* (containing "My Last Duchess" and "Soliloquy of the Spanish Cloister") and also of Tennyson's *Poems*, which included his dramatic monologues "Ulysses" and "St. Simeon Stylites." Before 1842 Browning had published the dramatic monologues "Porphyria's Lover" and "Johannes Agricola in Meditation" (1836), but again, Tennyson had been composing monologues since the late 1820s (e.g., "Remorse" and "St. Lawrence"). His poem "Supposed Confessions of a Second-rate Sensitive Mind not in Unity with Itself" (from *Poems, Chiefly Lyrical*, 1830) was probably given such an unwieldy title precisely in order to distinguish the speaker's voice from the poet's. Although Tennyson technically may have begun writing dramatic monologues a little before Browning, the latter's output in the form was eventually much greater.

In the latter half of the 19th century, after the publication of Tennyson's *Maud* and Browning's *Men and Women*, the dramatic monologue came into its own, and hundreds of them were composed. Faas, in the appendix to his book *Retreat into the Mind*, lists "practitioners of the dramatic monologue among minor Victorian poets" with the titles of scores of representative poems, largely forgotten today (Faas, 210–15). Among better-known late Victorians, Swinburne, William Morris, and the Rossettis all wrote dramatic monologues.

Various critics have theorized why the dramatic monologue flourished so in the mid-19th century. For Langbaum the form represents a development of dramatic elements present in Romantic lyrics of the early 19th century. He sees the dramatic monologue as a "poetry of sympathy" in which the reader is given "facts from within"; and he considers that the Romantic poet, no longer able, as in previous centuries, to rely on absolute values or moral standards, posits instead his own experience as a yardstick and later, by extension, tries—in the dramatic monologue—to enter sympathetically into the subjective experience of others (Langbaum, 78–79, 160, 167–68). Yet Blake and Burns, not to mention Chaucer and others, seem to have felt sufficient sympathy with their speakers to compose in their names poems that amount to dramatic monologues, without the benefit of the Romantic lyric behind them.

Langbaum's view also tends to conflate the greater Romantic lyric and the dramatic monologue, seeing both as a "poetry of experience," rather than stressing the distinction between them, namely that the "I" of the Romantic lyric expresses—or may, and very often does, express—the poet's own self, whereas the "I" of the dramatic monologue explicitly seeks to avoid subjective expression. Tennyson complained in a note to "Locksley Hall Sixty Years After" that readers and reviewers tended "to regard each poem and story as a story of the poet's life." It seems very likely that one attraction of the dramatic monologue, for poets succeeding the Romantics, must have been to make such an error impossible, or more difficult: to avoid the confessional nature of the Romantic "I" without forgoing the reader-sympathy associated with first-person discourse. Arguing against this notion that Browning "developed the dramatic monologue as a means of escaping from the inherited condition of Romantic subjectivity," Slinn contends that Browning "uses his personae to dramatise subjectivity, not to avoid it" (Slinn, 8). It is true, as we have seen, that Browning explores the difficulties inherent in understanding and expressing the self; nevertheless, he specifically avoids using his own subjectivity in illustration of those difficulties, choosing to do so instead with the "utterances of so many imaginary persons, not mine." As Carol T. Christ points out, by detaching "these 'utterances' from his own person, he avoids presenting problems of self-consciousness in his own voice, but he remains preoccupied with such problems in the voices he creates."[22] He may be using his personae to "dramatise subjectivity", but it is not his own subjectivity that he dramatizes—except to the extent that all literary creations ultimately spring from the imaginations of their authors and, therefore, involve self-dramatization at some level.

The adoption of the dramatic monologue form suggests a deliberate will to avoid self-expression as far as possible, even though the poet's voice, as we know, cannot fail to be heard behind that of the speaker. It goes without saying, too, that the author of a dramatic monologue may sometimes deliberately put his own opinions or feelings into the mouths of his personae, just as a novelist or dramatist may do. Thus Fra Lippo Lippi expresses views on art known to have been held by Browning. This in itself does not make the poem subjective, since Browning has taken the trouble to set up the character of his protagonist and establish the context as that of Renaissance Italy.

Other critics have looked elsewhere than in Romantic poetry to find reasons for the sudden popularity of the dramatic monologue in the mid-19th century. A. Dwight Culler sees a possible source in monodrama (Culler, 368–69). Philip Hobsbaum regards the flowering of the dramatic monologue as connected with a growing tendency to value soliloquies above action in the theater—a tendency he sees as a major reason for the decline of drama after the age of Shakespeare. Individual speeches became more important to both playwrights and spectators than the plot as a whole, and were often appreciated independently of their context. This shift gave rise to the publication of various popular anthologies of speeches extracted from plays, such as Dr. Dodd's *The Beauties of Shakespeare* (1752) and Lamb's *Specimens of English Dramatic Poets* (1808)—speeches that, if not too dependent on their dramatic context, can sound much like the poems we call dramatic monologues. Hobsbaum points out that when Lamb's enormously popular *Specimens* came out in 1808, relatively few monologues had been composed, whereas "the next generation, that of Browning and Tennyson, was prolific in the form"; and he posits a probable connection between this sudden proliferation of the dramatic monologue and "the anthologists' way of reading drama as isolated scenes, as 'beauties.'"[23] A climate in which it is considered preferable to read or recite an isolated soliloquy, rather than watch the play performed in its entirety on the stage, must be inherently conducive to the writing of dramatic monologues.

Faas also sees stage plays, specifically Shakespeare's, as an important ancestor of the 19th-century dramatic monologue. Like Langbaum, he considers the greater Romantic lyric as one source, along with "Shakespeare's psychological realism, particularly in his soliloquies" (Faas, 103). Noting that the most common name for a dramatic monologue before that term became current was "psychological monologue," and that Browning was considered the poet of psychology, Faas links the flowering of the dramatic monologue, as his subtitle indicates, with the rise of psychiatry in the 19th century. He remarks that Victorian critics appreciated the psychological depth of Browning's dramatic monologues (whose stress lay, as the poet himself claims in a preface to *Sordello*, "on the incidents in the development of a soul"); and that they saw Browning as a successor of Shakespeare in this respect.

In connection with Shakespeare, Faas raises another interesting question concerning the dramatic monologue: "Why should such a genre originate in England, but not in non-English-speaking countries? . . . Why . . . did there arise a school of dramatic-psychological poetry in the English language alone?" The answer, he says, lies in the familiarity of English poets with Shakespeare, whose "realistic use of language . . . and general insight into the human mind became models for the Victorian authors of dramatic monologues" (Faas, 105). He comments that contemporary reviewers took this influence for granted.

### The dramatic monologue in other national literatures

In literatures other than English and American one finds only isolated examples of dramatic monologues. The form is virtually unknown in Russian, Italian, Spanish, and French literature.

In spite of Pushkin's narrative and dramatic genius, as evidenced in his novel in verse, *Eugene Onegin,* and several poems in dialogue form such as "Mozart and Salerij," he did not write any dramatic monologues, nor can I find examples among other Russian poets.

In Italian poetry the lyric impulse is much stronger than the dramatic, with the notable exception of Dante's *Divine Comedy.* The *Inferno,* a dramatic narrative in verse, introduces a series of characters who successively relate their stories. The speakers are in hell as a punishment for their sins, yet they try to present themselves in an attractive light—a procedure resembling that of Browning's dramatic monologues. Indeed, Dante may have played a part, along with Chaucer and Shakespeare, in molding Browning's dramatic awareness.[24]

German poetry boasts a form much like the dramatic monologue, namely the *Rollengedicht* or "role-poem" mentioned above in connection with the narrative and fictional characteristics of the dramatic monologue. The definition of a *Rollengedicht*, however, is *"Empfindungen und Gedenken einer typischen Gestalt,"* or "feelings and thoughts of a typical figure," such as a lover, wanderer, soldier, shepherd, and so on. The accent on typicality results in poems that could be spoken by *any* lover, *any* soldier, or *any* shepherd. Examples of the *Rollengedicht* are Goethe's "Shepherd's Complaint"; Brentano's "Spinner's Song"; Uhland's "Boy's Mountain Song"; and Mörike's "The Forsaken Girl," who weeps as she gazes into the fire and remembers that she has dreamed all night long of her faithless beloved. Rilke wrote a series of poems in this form: for example, "The Beggar's Song," "The Widow's Song," "The Idiot's Song," "The Suicide's Song," and "The Blind Man's Song." They are moving and dramatic; the blind man, for example, is angry as well as unhappy: "I am blind, you out there. That is a curse, / An abomination, a contradiction, / A daily weight";[25] nevertheless, this poem could be spoken by any blind man, the "Beggar's Song" by any beggar, and so on. The speaker of a *Rollengedicht* does have a certain identity, dependent on his profession (e.g., soldier, shepherd) or other activity (e.g., wanderer, lover), but because of their typicality, these speakers are not far removed from the unidentified "I" of the lyric poem. By contrast, the speakers of the English dramatic monologues we shall examine are identified as individuals and placed in a specific, unique context.

The dramatic monologue is virtually unknown in Spanish poetry, too. The Spanish Romantic poet José de Espronceda wrote a few monologues that resemble the German *Rollengedicht* in that the speaker is a typical, rather than a specific, particularized figure; indeed, it may have been de Espronceda's reading of German poetry that led him to write his "Pirate's Song" and the songs of "The Beggar" and "The Executioner". These poems are monologues, although again they could be spoken by any pirate or rebel, any beggar, any executioner.[26]

Modern Polish poetry boasts several dramatic monologues among the works of Zbigniew Herbert and Czeslaw Milosz. In Herbert's "Elegy of Fortinbras," Fortinbras addresses the dead Hamlet, who "chose the easier part an elegant thrust" whereas he must deal with the mundane tasks of government, such as "a decree on prostitutes and beggars" and a "better system of prisons." In "The Divine Claudius," the Roman Emperor denies the charge of cruelty usually made against him, declaring that "in reality I was only absent-minded"; for example, "sometimes it would happen I invited / the dead to a game of dice," even though he himself had ordered these deaths. He justifies his actions by suggesting that "the goal of these operations was sublime / I longed to make death familiar to people / to dull its edge."

Another poem, "Damastes (Also Known as Procrustes) Speaks," features the inventor of the Procrustean bed, who in the tradition of the dramatic monologue, attempts to excuse his actions. He was trying to construct men of perfect size: "I invented a bed with the measurements of a perfect man / I compared the travelers I caught with this bed." Of course, since they did not all fit, he had to cut legs here and there, or stretch them, and then the people died; but he continued to believe in his research: "the goal was noble progress demands victims." This belief that the ends justify the means is one source of the woes of 20th-century societies under totalitarian regimes, as Herbert well knew, having lived under Communist rule as well as through the Second World War. Much of Herbert's poetry has political undertones, both the dramatic monologues and his other poems. Stanislaw Baranczak cites Browning and the Greek poet Cavafy as models for Herbert's dramatic monologues.[27] Cafavy's works do include monologues spoken by figures from Greek history, though one often feels, especially in the love poetry, that the distance between the speaker and the poet's persona is not very great.

The works of another Polish poet, Czeslaw Milosz, who emigrated to the United States in 1960, include several dramatic monologues. His *Collected Poems 1931–1987*—a selection of his poetry translated into English—contains the "Song of a Citizen," in the "Voices of Poor People" section; and the "Songs of Adrian Zielinski," set in Warsaw in the "fifth spring of war." For these poems the author provided the following note: "Adrian Zielinski is a fictitious name, like J. Alfred Prufrock"—which places them firmly in the dramatic monologue tradition. In French there is no name available for this kind of poem; the term "*monologue dramatique*" refers to a monologue in a stage play. In medieval studies, it denotes a comic monologue performed by a single actor at a market or fair. Even in the 19th century, dramatic monologues in French are practically non-existent. Alfred de Vigny, who prided himself on the "*forme Epique ou Dramatique*" of his *Poèmes antiques et modernes*, came very close to the dramatic monologue form with works like "Moise" ("Moses"), "La Colère de Samson" ("Samson's Anger"), or "Le Mont des Oliviers" ("The Mount of Olives"), whose speakers are, respectively, Moses, Samson, and Christ; but all these poems comprise introductions or conclusions of varying lengths presenting or commenting on the speaker, rather than the totally independent speech of a persona. It can be argued that Mallarmé's *L'Après-midi d'un faune* (*The Afternoon of a Faun*) and Valéry's *La Jeune Parque* (*The Young Fate*), as well as other poems of his, are dramatic monologues, albeit of a totally different kind from Browning's.[28] The speakers of these poems, though identified as other than the poet, are not characterized at all; the drama involves no conflict between speaker and world, as is usually the case in Browning, but is almost totally internal, the persona wrestling with his or her own psyche; finally the language of these poems, involved, complex, and highly poetic, is far removed from Browning's racy colloquial style. In all these respects the French dramatic monologues resemble the world of French classical drama, as epitomized in the plays of Racine, in contrast to the theater of Shakespeare. With Mallarmé and Valéry we move in a Racinian universe, an ahistorical world of myth, whose protagonists are universal figures engaged in inner conflict and speak a stylized language of their own.

Now, since the dramatic monologue presents a character's speech—or sometimes his thoughts—it lends itself to being written in the style of oral discourse (though not necessarily, as we saw with Tennyson). Many English and American poets—especially since Browning—prefer to adopt the accents of normal speech as the language of poetry, which, according to Ezra Pound should depart "in no way from speech save by heightened intensity." Eliot criticized Valéry for "assimilating poetry to music," thereby failing "to insist upon its relation to speech."[29]

Even in his *Four Quartets* (not a dramatic monologue), the intonations are those of a speaking voice, which retains the rhythms
and syntactical constructions of oral speech even when treating
the most abstract or literary topics, as in this extract from "Burnt
Norton":

> . . . Except for the point, the still point,
> There would be no dance, and there is only the dance.
> I can only say, *there* we have been: but I cannot say where.
> And I cannot say, how long, for that is to place it in time.

In Valéry's *La Jeune Parque*, in contrast, the frequent use of
inversion alone suffices to distance this language from that
of normal speech, likening it, in some degree, to the language of
Racine. And despite a few exceptions such as Laforgue, Corbière,
Max Jacob, Prévert, and Queneau, who use the diction of everyday speech in their poetry, most 19th- and 20th-century French
poets, like Mallarmé and Valéry, regard the language of poetry
as separate and different from oral discourse, and choose a "written" rather than a spoken style. Gerald Bruns comments on "the
contrast between Mallarmé's typographical efforts to escape the
lyricism of the human voice . . . and Wallace Stevens' conception
of 'speaking humanly'"; and Robert Greene notes that modern
French poets "continue the progressive purification of poetry
that began with Baudelaire, a process of ascesis whose goal has
been to strip from poetry all that is non-poetic, such as conventional prosody, narrative development and moral or ideological
concerns, so as to get at 'la poésie pure.'"[30]

French poets such as Reverdy, Saint John Perse, René Char,
Aragon, Bonnefoy, Du Bouchet, Francis Ponge, and Jacques
Dupin tend to use language that could only be written, not spoken. Apart from a general avoidance of colloquialisms or conversational turns of phrase, the cross-references, the sheer accumu-
lation of images, and in some cases the syntax, render this poetry
too dense to represent anyone's spoken utterance. For such
poets the dramatic monologue must appear a less attractive form
than for those who like to base their poetic diction on speech.

Another possible advantage of the dramatic monologue, since
it evokes the presence of a speaker, is the opportunity it affords
the poet—should he wish to avail himself of it—for characterization. Again, interest in character for its own sake seems more

typical of English and American literature than of French, as it is more typical of Shakespeare than of Racine.

For Victorian readers, one attraction of the dramatic monologue form was undoubtedly character portrayal; they appreciated complex psychological analyses on the model of Shakespeare. We have seen already in Browning, however, doubts about the possibility of self-expression, and also that the individual's estimation of his own experience and worth is not necessarily valid. His personae, like the Duke of Ferrara, act out a part, in an attempt to impose on their interlocutors their own view of themselves. By the 20th century the notion of selfhood was being questioned widely; personality was seen as split or multiple, as a matter of role-playing. Many poets use the dramatic monologue as a way of exploring such issues. The split in Prufrock's personality is expressed in the poem's first line; and he is ready to act his part, to "prepare a face to meet the faces that you meet."

The dramatic impulse remains strong in 20th-century poetry, especially in the United States. A few poets avoid the dramatic monologue altogether in favor of the lyric "I" of so-called confessional poetry; but many prominent 20th-century poets produce, in addition to lyrics, poems in the dramatic mode, whether dialogues or monologues. We will find examples of the dramatic monologue in the works of Ezra Pound, E.A. Robinson, Robert Lowell, Robert Frost, Randall Jarrell, Richard Howard, and other major 20th-century poets.

First, however, let us examine in detail dramatic monologues by the most famous practitioners of the form: Browning and Tennyson.

# Chapter 2

# THE VICTORIANS

### Robert Browning

To illustrate some of the questions raised in the foregoing chapter I have chosen one of Browning's most typical and well-known monologues, "The Bishop Orders His Tomb at Saint Praxed's Church," published in *Dramatic Romances and Lyrics* (1845). Other poems could have served: "Fra Lippo Lippi" or "Andrea del Sarto"—but both of these are rather long; "My Last Duchess"—but it has been much discussed already;[1] "Soliloquy of the Spanish Cloister" or "Porphyria's Lover"—but they are not quite as typical, or as rich in detail, as "The Bishop Orders His Tomb."

Browning (1812–1889) took quite a while to arrive at the dramatic monologue form. Before *Dramatic Romances and Lyrics*, he had already published some long poems and several plays, none of which was ever very successful. In the preface to one of these plays, *Strafford* (1837), he declared that it illustrated "Action in Character," rather than the "Character in Action" one usually expects in a stage play. His first dramatic monologues had appeared (together with other poems) in an earlier collection, *Dramatic Lyrics* (1842), and he was much more successful with this form, which permits action in character without needing to show characters in action, on the stage.

This chapter gives a short presentation of "The Bishop Orders His Tomb," followed by an analysis of the poem in the light of various issues concerning the dramatic monologue form discussed in Chapter 1.

THE BISHOP ORDERS HIS TOMB AT SAINT PRAXED'S
CHURCH
ROME, 15—

Vanity, saith the preacher, vanity!
Draw round my bed: is Anselm keeping back?
Nephews-sons mine . . . ah God, I know not! Well—
She, men would have to be your mother once,
Old Gandolf envied me, so fair she was!                  5
What's done is done, and she is dead beside,
Dead long ago, and I am Bishop since,
And as she died so must we die ourselves,
And thence ye may perceive the world's a dream.
Life, how and what is it? As here I lie                  10
In this state-chamber, dying by degrees,
Hours and long hours in the dead night, I ask
"Do I live, am I dead?" Peace, peace seems all.
Saint Praxed's ever was the church for peace;
And so, about this tomb of mine. I fought                15
With tooth and nail to save my niche, ye know:
—Old Gandolf cozened me, despite my care;
Shrewd was that snatch from out the corner South
He graced his carrion with, God curse the same!
Yet still my niche is not so cramped but thence          20
One sees the pulpit o'the epistle-side,
And somewhat of the choir, those silent seats,
And up into the aery dome where live
The angels, and a sunbeam's sure to lurk:
And I shall fill my slab of basalt there,                25
And 'neath my tabernacle take my rest,
With those nine columns round me, two and two,
The odd one at my feet where Anselm stands;

Peach-blossom marble all, the rare, the ripe
As fresh-poured red wine of a mighty pulse. 30
—Old Gandolf with his paltry onion-stone,
Put me where I may look at him! True peach,
Rosy and flawless: how I earned the prize!
Draw close: that conflagration of my church
—What then: So much was saved if aught were missed! 35
My sons, ye would not be my death? Go dig
The white-grape vineyard where the oil-press stood,
Drop water gently till the surface sinks,
And if ye find . . . ah God, I know not, I! . . .
Bedded in store of rotten fig-leaves soft, 40
And corded up in a tight olive-frail,
Some lump, ah God, of *lapis lazuli*,
Big as a Jew's head cut off at the nape,
Blue as a vein o'er the Madonna's breast—
Sons, all have I bequeathed you, villas, all, 45
That brave Frascati villa with its bath—
So, let the blue lump poise between my knees,
Like God the Father's globe on both his hands
Ye worship in the Jesu Church so gay,
For Gandolf shall not choose but see and burst! 50
Swift as a weaver's shuttle fleet our years;
Man goeth to the grave, and where is he?
Did I say basalt for my slab, sons? Black—
'Twas ever antique-black I meant! How else
Shall ye contrast my frieze to come beneath? 55
The bas-relief in bronze ye promised me,
Those Pans and Nymphs ye wot of, and perchance
Some tripod, thyrsus, with a vase or so,
The Saviour at his sermon on the mount,
St. Praxed in a glory, and one Pan 60
Ready to twitch the Nymph's last garment off,
And Moses with the tables . . . but I know
Ye mark me not! What do they whisper thee,
Child of my bowels, Anselm? Ah, ye hope
To revel down my villas while I gasp 65
Bricked o'er with beggar's moldy travertine
Which Gandolf from his tomb-top chuckles at!
Nay, boys, ye love me-all of jasper, then!
'Tis jasper ye stand pledged to, lest I grieve
My bath must needs be left behind, alas! 70
One block, pure green as a pistachio-nut,
There's plenty jasper somewhere in the world—

And have I not St. Praxed's ear to pray
Horses for ye, and brown Greek manuscripts,
And mistresses with great smooth marbly limbs?          75
—That's if ye carve my epitaph aright,
Choice Latin, picked phrase, Tully's every word,
No gaudy ware like Gandolf's second line—
Tully, my masters? Ulpian serves his need!
And then how I shall lie through centuries,          80
And hear the blessed mutter of the mass,
And see God made and eaten all day long,
And feel the steady candle-flame, and taste
Good strong thick stupefying incense-smoke!
For as I lie here, hours of the dead night,          85
Dying in state and by such slow degrees,
I fold my arms as if they clasped a crook,
And stretch my feet forth straight as stone can point
And let the bedclothes for a mortcloth drop
Into great laps and folds of sculptor's-work:          90
And as yon tapers dwindle, and strange thoughts
Grow, with a certain humming in my ears,
About the life before I lived this life,
And this life too, popes, cardinals and priests,
Saint Praxed at his sermon on the mount,          95
Your tall pale mother with her talking eyes,
And new-found agate urns as fresh as day,
And marble's language, Latin pure, discreet,
—Aha, ELUCESCEBAT quoth our friend?
No Tully, said I, Ulpian at the best!          100
Evil and brief hath been my pilgrimage.
All lapis, all, sons! Else I give the Pope
My villas: will ye ever eat my heart:
Ever your eyes were as a lizard's quick,
They glitter like your mother's for my soul,          105
Or ye would heighten my impoverished frieze,
Piece out its starved design, and fill my vase
With grapes, and add a vizor and a Term,
And to the tripod ye would tie a lynx
That in his struggle throws the thyrsus down,          110
To comfort me on my entablature
Whereon I am to lie till I must ask
"Do I live, am I dead?" There, leave me, there!
For ye have stabbed me with ingratitude
To death-ye wish it-God, ye wish it! Stone—          115
Gritstone, a-crumble! Clammy squares which sweat

As if the corpse they keep were oozing through—
And no more *lapis* to delight the world!
Well, go! I bless ye. Fewer tapers there,
But in a row: and, going, turn your backs          120
—Ay, like departing altar-ministrants,
And leave me in my church, the church for peace,
That I may watch at leisure if he leers—
Old Gandolf, at me, from his onion-stone,
As still he envied me, so fair she was!

The title of a dramatic monologue usually offers valuable information concerning the speaker's identity or situation. It often gives his/her name, as in "Fra Lippo Lippi," "Andrea del Sarto," "Ulysses," or "The Love Song of J. Alfred Prufrock." Browning's original title for this poem was simply "The Tomb at Saint Praxed's," but he no doubt found that too anonymous. The present title still does not name the Bishop; however, it is more important in this instance for the reader to know his profession than his name. We are presented here not with a historical individual, as in the case of the painter Andrea del Sarto, but with a *representative* of an era. And of what era? That information is provided by the mention "ROME, 15—" following the title. Renaissance Italy: an era that witnessed the rebirth of science, letters, art and music; an age of beauty, of great pictures by world-renowned masters; but also a time of luxury and decadence, of struggles for power and rivalry between noble families, of domination by the Catholic church, and of corruption in high places. The nineteenth-century art critic Ruskin admired Browning's poem for capturing "the Renaissance spirit,—its worldliness, inconsistency, pride, hypocrisy, ignorance of itself, love of art, of luxury, and of good Latin."[2]

One additional detail of the poem's title is informative: the Bishop is ordering his tomb, which suggests that he has not long to live. The name of his church, Saint Praxed's, is confirmed in line 14, and he refers several times in the course of the poem to the saint herself, who lived in Rome in the first century A.D.

The poem opens with a famous text from Ecclesiastes 1: "Vanity, saith the preacher, vanity!" Clearly such a quotation is suitable in the mouth of a bishop, especially a bishop on his deathbed, yet subsequent details reveal that the Bishop does not by any means regard the values and trappings of earthly life as "vain." The first line acts as an ironic commentary in advance of the Bishop's monologue, which will show him to be a man consumed by greed and vanity. The text is probably one the Bishop used to quote in his sermons and that he throws out now unthinkingly.

Like many dramatic monologues, this one begins *in medias res:* since it represents an extract from an on-going conversation, there is no introduction or exposition, and the reader has to puzzle out the dynamics of the situation from clues provided later. We know the Bishop is dying, so that the "Draw round my bed" comes as no surprise; but to whom is he saying that? The following line suggests an answer—"Nephews—sons mine . . . "—but at the same time poses a new question: are these young men the Bishop's sons or his nephews? Obviously, as a man of the Church, the Bishop can have only illegitimate sons, and he has probably had them brought up as his nephews, yet on his deathbed he wants to acknowledge their true relationship. Still he cannot bring himself quite to admit it: he refers to their mother as "She, men would have to be your mother once." He is proud of her beauty, however, which was envied by a rival clergyman, Old Gandolf, who may well have been the Bishop's predecessor as Bishop of Saint Praxed's. One of the sons, Anselm, appears to be his father's favorite, since the Bishop mentions him alone by name, several times in the course of the poem.

Reflecting on his mistress's death leads the Bishop to utter more platitudes that he does not take seriously: "thence ye may perceive the world's a dream," he says, yet we will find that he is very attached to this world; and his declaration "Peace, peace seems all. / Saint Praxed's ever was the church for peace" is immediately contradicted by a statement that has the ring of truth: "I fought / With tooth and nail to save my niche, ye know." As a clergyman, he has learned to preach about "Peace," but as with the text on vanity, he does not take his own preaching to heart.

By now (line 15) he has arrived at the topic he wishes to discuss—not for the first time—with his sons: the question of his tomb. Old Gandolf has a tomb the Bishop scorns as being of "paltry onion-stone," a cheap marble, so called because it peeled easily. His own must be so splendid that all the world, and Old Gandolf in particular, will envy it. He covets an elaborate edifice with a basalt slab (which he later alters to the more valuable "antique-black," ll. 53–54); nine columns of "Peach-blossom marble"; a lump of precious lapis lazuli (which he stole from the church during a fire and hid in a vineyard); a frieze (l. 55); and an epitaph carved in "Choice Latin" (ll. 76–77), by which he means Cicero ("Tully"), whereas Ulpian, a later and inferior writer, was good enough for Gandolf (ll. 79, 100). The Bishop is aware, however, that his sons might not comply with his wishes; they might brick him over "with beggar's mouldy travertine" (limestone) or give him "Stone— / Gritstone, a-crumble!" He would like to believe that his sons love him enough to carry out his instructions ("Nay boys, ye love me—all of jasper, then!"), but realizes in his more lucid moments that they will not (" . . . ye have stabbed me with ingratitude / To death—ye wish it—God, ye wish it!"). Therefore he attempts to blackmail them by threatening to bequeath his villas to the Pope instead of them (ll. 102–3) and offering to pray to Saint Praxed for horses for them, and "mistresses with great smooth marbly limbs."

Relating this poem to our earlier discussion of the dramatic monologue, we see that it has the objective quality (that Browning called "dramatic") essential to the genre: the Bishop speaks throughout, and he is clearly identified as an autonomous figure with a recognizable personality. As a churchman, he has at his command a fund of biblical quotations and Christian allusions that he is in the habit of citing—but without reflecting on them. "Swift as a weaver's shuttle fleet our years," he pronounces, quoting Job 7, "Man goeth to the grave, and where is he?" Instead of contemplating this question, however, he returns at once to the topic of his magnificent tomb, without seeing the irony involved in this shift. True, he is on his deathbed, and his mind sometimes wanders: he often does not complete his sentences (ll. 59–69), and he confuses Saint Praxed with Christ (l. 95), and makes the Saint male instead of female. But one has the impression that he was never much of a thinker: what counts for him is material splendor rather than any intellectual or spiritual values. His religion depends on the senses, not the spirit. For example, he describes how he will

> . . . . . . . . . . . lie through centuries,
> And hear the blessed mutter of the mass,
> And see God made and eaten all day long,
> And feel the steady candle-flame, and taste
> Good strong thick stupefying incense-smoke!

In the face of imminent death, he is concerned not with the fate of his immortal soul, but with the appearance of his tomb. Indeed, his view of immortality seems confined to a vision of his present bedridden state continuing "through centuries": ". . . let the bedclothes, for a mortcloth, drop / Into great laps and folds of sculptor's-work" (ll. 89–90). Immortality for him is connected, not with a spiritual life, but with the durability of the stone he would choose for his tomb. Marble, jasper, and *lapis lazuli* will guarantee him eternal life, it seems, in contrast to the porous "mouldy travertine" or coarse-grained "Gritstone, a-crumble" that he is afraid his ungenerous sons will provide.

Other details reveal his aesthetic delight in expensive items: the pillars surrounding his tomb should be "Peach-blossom marble all, the rare, the ripe / As fresh-poured red wine of a mighty pulse / . . . True peach, / Rosy and flawless." His sensuous description of the *lapis lazuli* is emphasized by the interjection "ah God" (l. 42) and the comparison "Blue as a vein o'er the Madonna's breast." A certain callousness also comes out in the preceding line ("Big as a Jew's head cut off at the nape"). His greed for precious stones and objects is not confined to the decoration of his tomb; one of his greatest regrets at leaving this world is that he will lose his "bath" (probably a pool): "One block, pure green as a pistachio nut." Park Honan has shown how the Bishop's sensuousness is suggested by his use of color.[3]

Not only does the Bishop emphasize material over spiritual values, he also confuses Christian and pagan motifs in his suggestions for decorating the tomb:

> Those Pans and Nymphs ye wot of, and perchance
> Some tripod, thyrsus, with a vase or so,
> The Saviour at his sermon on the mount,
> Saint Praxed in a glory, and one Pan
> Ready to twitch the Nymph's last garment off . . . .

Browning always takes care to place his speakers in a detailed spatial and temporal context, providing them with a realistic background. The date "15—" and the Bishop's Renaissance attitudes and values establish the era in which he lived; the subtitle also specifies that we are in Rome, and the Bishop makes various references to things Italian, such as grapes, olives, figs, "popes, cardinals and priests" and his "Frascati villa," Frascati being a town near Rome. The impression of location in a specific setting is enhanced in the poem by the use of *deictics*—words like the demonstrative adjective "this" or the adverbs "here" or "now," which imply presence in an actual, particular scene. The Bishop mentions "this state-chamber" (l. 11), and says "as I lie here" (l. 85) or "as yon tapers dwindle" (l. 91). Such phrases are commonly used in dramatic monologues to draw the reader into the scene and increase its immediacy.

By particularizing his speaker and placing him in a specific historical setting, Browning endows him with a separate existence of his own, thus establishing his distance both from himself and from the reader—a distance characteristic of the dramatic monologue in which the "I" of the speaker is identified as Other.

All the realistic detail that Browning supplies as context for his protagonists prompts the reader to regard them as characters in a fiction, since the procedure of identifying characters and placing them in a certain setting is typical of narrative fiction. Thus we find critics asserting that "it is as novels . . . that many of Browning's poems offer themselves."[4] Indeed, Browning's dramatic monologues have an important narrative dimension; his speakers have a past, a story that unfolds as the poem progresses. The Bishop, we know, had a mistress when he was younger, and has several sons by her; she died long ago and subsequently he became Bishop; a fire in his church (which he may have started himself) enabled him to steal and hide away the large piece of *lapis lazuli* that he would now like his sons to recover and use in his tomb. As in a novel, also, Browning's speakers usually present a well-defined, three-dimensional personality: "one whole man," as Pound was later to say of them in his *Three Cantos*. The question remains: does the Bishop of Saint Praxed's possess such individuality, or is he *merely* a representative of his age, of the "Renaissance spirit," as Ruskin says?

Tucker has suggested that the identity of the "I" in a dramatic monologue is threatened by two extremes: on the one hand, by being too little characterized—too close to the vague "I" of the lyric; and on the other, by being too representative of a particular era, "merely a tissue of affiliations."[5] The Bishop of Saint Praxed's, like most of Browning's speakers, easily escapes the former fate because Browning particularizes him in great detail; and regarding the other extreme, he is surely more than simply a "tissue" of 16th-century affiliations. His individuality comes out in his obsessive preoccupation with certain items, such as his bath and the "lump" of *lapis*, his rivalry with Old Gandolf, and his former mistress's beauty; and it is also apparent in his naiveté. On first reading the poem, one is tempted to label the Bishop a hypocrite; yet that term implies a level of sophisticated duplicity of which he seems incapable. His utter self-absorption has a childlike quality that the reader may find amusing rather than repugnant, and that helps to individualize him. Though faintly conscious of his most outrageous sins—hence his hesitation in naming his sons and in revealing the hiding place of the *lapis lazuli* he stole—he seems to feel no remorse for these sins; and he remains blissfully unaware of less tangible vices such as greed, envy and selfishness, lack of true spiritual faith, and sensuousness and materialism. He thinks of himself as a perfectly satisfactory clergyman; he has spent his life with "popes, cardinals and priests," listened to the "blessed mutter of the mass," and quoted the Bible; he feels he has "earned the prize" (l. 33) of an elegant tomb.

Thus the dramatic monologue, while presenting a fully rounded, lifelike character, simultaneously subverts the notion of personality and the possibility of its reliable expression, by revealing how partial any view of character tends to be. As Clyde de L. Ryals points out, "any point of view is necessarily partial (in both meanings of the word) and therefore suspect and unreliable."[6] The dual voice characteristic of the dramatic monologue allows us simultaneously to hear the Bishop pleading his case and the poet condemning him.

Browning achieves this split by his attention to linguistic detail. The Bishop betrays himself by exclamations and hesitations (for example, ll. 3, 39, 42, 68), and by his ironic juxtapositions (ll. 14–15, 51–53, 60–62). His choice of words often reveals where his true values lie, as with the "Peach-blossom marble" or the "lump" of *lapis*. The extraordinary variety of his vocabulary reflects his preoccupation with stones: basalt, marble, onionstone, *lapis lazuli*, travertine, jasper, gritstone. . . . Certain words are repeated several times to indicate his obsession, for example, bath, jasper, marble, and *lapis*. Browning also uses alliteration to emphasize the Bishop's covetousness. The evocative rolling of *p* and *r* sounds in lines 29–30 suggests the sensuous pleasure he takes in marble, and in wine: "Peach-blossom marble all, the rare, the ripe / as fresh-poured red wine of a mighty pulse." The repetition of *b* in "Big as a Jew's head . . . / Blue as a vein" reinforces these images, like the murmuring *m* sound in "blessed mutter of the mass" (l. 81). Again a sensuous pleasure emerges from the *m* and *b* sounds in "mistresses with great smooth marbly limbs" (l. 75); here the Bishop's obsession with marble combines with his appreciation of the female body. Sometimes the rhythm of a line can suggest an emphatically sensuous attitude, as in the line "Good strong thick stupefying incense-smoke!" with its multiple strong stresses.

The split in the voice of the dramatic monologue is inevitable, since the words of the poem belong simultaneously to the speaker and to the poet. Thus Robert Langbaum points out that in the dramatic monologue "there is at work . . . a consciousness . . . beyond what the speaker can lay claim to. This consciousness is the mark of the poet's projection into the poem; and is also the pole which attracts our projection, since we find in it the counterpart of our own consciousness."[7] The reader and the poet, in other words, are in collusion; together they judge the poem's speaker.

This collusion contributes to the dramatic quality of Browning's poems, constituting a kind of dramatic irony. This type of irony usually is associated with plays: a character on the stage remains ignorant of something in his own situation that the audience knows about. In Browning's dramatic monologues, the element that the protagonist fails to perceive is often an aspect of his own character: We see, for example, that the Duke of Ferrara is excessively proud, cruel, and jealous; but that is not *his* view. Similarly, the Bishop of Saint Praxed's reveals a worldliness and vanity of which he remains unconscious.

Drama involves conflict, and this clash in views represents one kind of conflict in Browning's dramatic monologues. Very often his protagonists are also in conflict with another person or with society as a whole. The Bishop of Saint Praxed's struggles with his sons: if only he could persuade them to agree to build his elaborate tomb, he could die happy! No internal conflicts affect the Bishop—with his conscience, for example; Browning's characters look outward, and they grapple with the outside world. He usually places them in a "dramatic" or tense situation whose outcome could have considerable impact on their lives. Thus Fra Lippo Lippi has just been arrested, the Duke of Ferrara is planning a marriage, and the Bishop of Saint Praxed's is on his deathbed. The result of his attempt to convince his "nephews" will not affect his life; but his posthumous status, so important to him, depends on it.

Some critics deny that the speakers of Browning's monologues really intend to influence their interlocutors. Langbaum speaks of "character as song," maintaining that Browning's protagonists "never accomplish anything by their utterance, and seem to know from the start that they will not"; they are simply carried away by their own rhetoric. But it seems hard to imagine the Duke of Ferrara allowing himself to be carried away by a lyrical impulse simply "because one utterance engenders another," as Ryals puts it (Langbaum, 183; Ryals, 150–51). An arrogant aristocrat like the Duke, given the historical context and his place in society—and the place of women in that society—might well consider himself justified, for the reasons he gives, in murdering (or somehow brutally silencing) his former wife; and perhaps he wishes to notify his second wife, through the envoy, of the kind of behavior he expects from her. As for speakers like Andrea del Sarto and the Bishop of Saint Praxed's, they may be aware that they might achieve nothing by their utterance, but they persist, weakly, "hoping against hope" that they will succeed in persuading Lucrezia and the "nephews," respectively, to comply with their wishes.

Another dramatic aspect of Browning's poems lies in the fact that they are not really monologues, but dialogues, that is, the speech of the poem is addressed to an auditor; and second-person address is the distinctive form of drama. The interlocutor's reply is not given in a dramatic monologue, though often the speaker reacts as if to an inaudible comment or gesture from him/her. Thus the Bishop interrupts himself to say: ". . . but I know / Ye mark me not! What do they whisper thee, / Child of my bowels, Anselm?" Toward the end, the sons are no doubt showing signs of restlessness, so the Bishop dismisses them: "Well go! I bless ye." He addresses his sons in the second person, as is normal in dialogue; and imperatives abound—another feature of second-person address: "Draw round my bed"; "Put me where I may look at him!"; "Go dig / The white-grape vineyard."

Dramatic, second-person address produces lively, animated speech. Because the dramatic monologue represents the utterance of a speaker, it allows the poet to introduce the rhythms and cadences of oral discourse. The Bishop's speech is in blank verse, like many of Browning's dramatic monologues, and the rhythm is basically iambic pentameters, though with frequent variations. Also, being an educated man and a preacher, the Bishop has a wide vocabulary. He can quote from the Bible, he uses religious or philosophical-sounding phrases ("Evil and brief hath been my pilgrimage"), he can sustain a lengthy, complex sentence (e.g., ll. 20–30; 104–13), and he asks rhetorical questions ("Life, how and what is it?"). Nevertheless, the overall impression is of oral speech. The regular rhythm of the blank verse is undermined constantly by *enjambment*—the "run-on" effect created when the sense of a line continues without interruption into the following one. In this poem, pauses in the middle of a line are as common as at the end. The loose, disjointed syntax typical of colloquial English allows the Bishop to jump from one topic to another or insert new ideas into his flow of thought. Also, his long periods often peter out, unfinished (ll. 62, 99), or he interrupts himself (l. 45), as people do in conversation. In general, Browning prefers paratactic sentence structures, which allow his speakers continually to add elements to their discourse, joined together by the conjunction "and," over complex syntactic sentences with many subordinate clauses. There are many examples of this in "The Bishop Orders His Tomb," particularly in lines 80–100, with their frequent repetition of "And." The many genuine questions addressed to his sons ("Did I say basalt for my slab, sons?") also convey the oral quality of this discourse, as do the Bishop's hesitations, exclamations, and interjections ("And if ye find . . . Ah God, I know not, I! . . ."; cf. also ll. 3, 35, 62, 63, 102–3, 114–15). His confusion and hesitations often are signaled by punctuation: ellipsis points and dashes abound in this poem, as in other dramatic monologues by Browning.

Some of the difficulty readers experienced—and still experience—in reading Browning relates, paradoxically, to his attempts to reproduce the language of conversation in verse. Digressions, interruptions, and repetitions that are typical of spoken language and easy to follow when supported by a speaker's intonation, gestures, or facial expressions become incoherent and confusing when transcribed onto the page. When digressions, disruptions, and long, loosely constructed sentences become too prevalent, the effect of spontaneous oral discourse is lost. This is not true of "The Bishop Orders His Tomb," but in some of Browning's later poetry, the reader is unable to grasp the import of such passages at first reading, whereas oral speech usually aims at immediate comprehension.

Readers of his day found Browning not only difficult to follow but shockingly "unpoetic." They were accustomed to a traditional poetic style, with a formal rather than a colloquial diction, and a sustained, logical syntax. Wordsworth had advocated the use of natural-sounding language in poetry, yet it is still a far cry from his verse to a line like "Nephews—sons mine . . . ah God, I know not! Well—," which must have seemed totally unpoetic to readers accustomed to thinking of poetry in terms of euphony and noble diction. Browning's style, because of its juxtapositions of literary and highly colloquial language, as well as other features, is often called *grotesque*—a term originating with the critic Walter Bagehot, who wrote a review of Browning's and Tennyson's poetry in which he distinguished between three poetic styles: the "pure" (represented by Milton and Wordsworth), the "ornate" (represented by Tennyson), and the "grotesque" (represented by Browning).[8]

Browning's technique of reproducing the flavor of oral speech in poetry was taken up with enthusiasm by later English and American poets. Pound and Eliot both admired this aspect of Browning's work, Eliot claiming that Browning was the only 19th-century poet "to devise a way of speech which might be useful for others" and that this was achieved largely through his "use of non-poetic material" and his insistence on the "relation of poetry to speech." Pound, too, considered that the language of poetry should depart "in no way from speech save by heightened intensity."[9]

We will eventually examine dramatic monologues by Eliot and Pound; however, let us now turn to a contemporary of Browning's, Alfred Tennyson, who began writing dramatic monologues at the same time (though he did not write as many), but composed them in a totally non-colloquial idiom.

## Lord Alfred Tennyson

Like Browning, Tennyson lived a long life (1809–1892) and his output was vast. He became Poet Laureate in 1850, and during the second half of the nineteenth century his poetry was immensely popular. Subsequently his reputation suffered:

readers detected in some of his verse a typically Victorian sentimentality or else a too-strident note of patriotism. Eventually,
however, it became clear that the whole opus should not be con-
demned because of a few poems, and the past thirty years have
seen a resurgence of interest in his work, and a reevaluation of
his poetry.

Many of Tennyson's works are extremely long and were written over considerable periods of time. *The Idylls of the King,* composed over a period of fifty years and based on the Arthurian
legends, comprises twelve long poems, most of which have
500–1,000 lines. *Maud* (1855), a poem of over 1,000 lines, is a kind
of extended dramatic monologue; Tennyson subtitled it a "monodrama" in which, he says, "different phases of passion in one
person take the place of different characters."[10] Another long and
very famous poem is *In Memoriam A.H.H.,* written in memory of
his close and very dear friend Arthur Henry Hallam, who died in
1833 at the age of twenty-two. They had been inseparable friends
at Cambridge; Robert Martin refers to their reciprocal attraction
as "falling in friendship," as one falls in love.[11] They had traveled
abroad together, and Hallam was engaged to Tennyson's sister
Emily. The loss of this friend was a shattering blow to Tennyson;
the poem expresses his grief and also his thoughts on the issue of
the immortality of the soul—a topic that, given the spread of theories of evolution, was being discussed with particular urgency
at the time.

Tennyson's work presents a wide variety of forms and topics.
In addition to the long poems mentioned above, there are many
short lyrics, some very famous and frequently anthologized,
such as "Break, Break, Break," "The Eagle," and "The Splendour
Falls." As Poet Laureate he also had to write occasional verse
reflecting contemporary events, such as the "Ode on the Death
of the Duke of Wellington" and "Britons, Guard Your Own."

Dramatic monologues represent only a fraction of Tennyson's
output, yet he wrote enough of them to be considered one of the
principal masters of the form. Some of his dramatic monologues
are "Saint Simeon Stylites," "Ulysses," "Tithonus," "Tiresias,"
"Locksley Hall," "Lucretius," "Northern Farmer (Old Style),"
"Northern Farmer (New Style)," "Rizpah," "Columbus," "Sir
John Oldcastle," and "Romney's Remorse." Other poems, such
as "Oenone," approximate dramatic monologues but cannot
strictly be classified as such because the speaker's voice is not

totally autonomous. *Maud*, subtitled "A Monodrama," is an extended dramatic monologue spoken by Maud's former lover, an unbalanced, even paranoiac figure.

Most of Tennyson's dramatic monologues are very different in tone and atmosphere from Browning's, though one or two share some Browningesque features. "Saint Simeon Stylites," though not published until 1842, was written by 1833—before Browning had published any dramatic monologues; yet it resembles Browning's poems closely in technique, in that the speaker gradually, and unintentionally, condemns himself out of his own mouth. He presents himself as a saint, but the reader soon sees that his exaggerated mortification of his own flesh has its source in pride, self-satisfaction, and a desire to outdo all others. Linda Hughes draws a parallel between this poem and "The Bishop Orders His Tomb," stressing that Tennyson was quite capable of writing a Browningesque dramatic monologue when he so wished.[12]

We have seen that Browning's dramatic monologues are composed in a conversational, even colloquial diction. This is not true at all of Tennyson in general, although two monologues are written not only in colloquial style but in the dialect of Lincolnshire, where Tennyson grew up. The first line of "Northern Farmer (Old Style)" reads: "Wheer 'asta beän saw long and meä liggin' [lying] 'ere aloän?" The two "Northern Farmer" poems show that Tennyson could write in colloquial diction when appropriate.

The poem we will examine, "Tithonus," while unmistakably a dramatic monologue, is very different from Browning's poetry. "Tithonus" was completed in 1859, but the first version of the poem, "Tithon," dates from 1833. Both "Tithon" and "Ulysses" were composed shortly after Hallam's death. Tennyson called "Tithonus" "originally a pendent," i.e., a companion-piece, to "Ulysses," and of the latter poem he explained that it "was written soon after Arthur Hallam's death, and gave my feeling about the need of going forward, and braving the struggle of life perhaps more simply than anything in 'In Memoriam'" (Hallam Tennyson, 459 and 196). The Ulysses of Tennyson's poem is an old man; he has returned from Troy after many adventures on the high seas, as related in Homer's *Odyssey*, to his wife Penelope and his country, Ithaca. But whereas Homer's Ulysses was pleased to be home, Tennyson's (who owes not a little to the figure of Ulysses in Dante's *Inferno*) is bored with his role as governor of his people; restless, he seeks further adventures: "I cannot rest from travel; I will drink / Life to the lees." He is determined to leave Ithaca once again: "my purpose holds / To sail beyond the sunset, and the baths / Of all the western stars, until I die." Some critics suggest that Ulysses' goal is death, but his sense of adventure and thirst for new experiences seem stronger than any death-wish: "'Tis not too late to seek a newer world," he declares; and he describes himself as "always roaming with a hungry heart" and as "yearning in desire / To follow knowledge like a sinking star, / Beyond the utmost bound of human thought." He is anxious to achieve "Some work of noble note," before death.[13] Lines like these clearly relate to Tennyson's "need of going forward, and braving the struggle of life." Critics have suggested that, far from sympathizing with Ulysses' "noble" desire to fulfill himself by setting out on his travels once more, we should condemn him for abandoning his "aged wife" and his people, and for his condescending tone toward Telemachus.[14] In my view, however, the whole tone of the poem celebrates Ulysses' single-mindedness and determination, and reinforces the nobility inherent in sailing "beyond the sunset, and the baths / Of all the western stars."

If Ulysses wants to grasp whatever life may have left to offer, in the short time left to him, Tithonus, on the contrary, has all eternity before him but cannot grasp what he wants. This poem—or its original version—is a "pendent" to "Ulysses" in the aftermath of Hallam's death in that they present opposite attitudes. Ulysses reflects Tennyson's "need of going forward"; but Tithonus wants to die, an impulse that Tennyson, in his grief, also felt. This impulse can be seen, for example, in his poem "The Two Voices," begun in 1833 and originally entitled "Thoughts of a Suicide."

"Tithonus" is based on the Homeric myth (contained in his *Hymn to Aphrodite*), in which Eos, goddess of the dawn, in love with a mortal, Tithonus, obtained immortality for him from Zeus. In making the request, however, she failed to ask also for eternal youth, so that Tithonus gradually grew old, wrinkled, and impotent. The poem assumes that Tithonus has reached a point where he would rather die than endure the torment of seeing the beautiful Eos each day without being able to love her.

## TITHONUS

The woods decay, the woods decay and fall,
The vapours weep their burthen to the ground,
Man comes and tills the field and lies beneath,
And after many a summer dies the swan.
Me only cruel immortality                                             5
Consumes: I wither slowly in thine arms,
Here at the quiet limit of the world,
A white-hair'd shadow roaming like a dream
The ever-silent spaces of the East,
Far-folded mists, and gleaming halls of morn.            10
Alas! for this gray shadow, once a man—
So glorious in his beauty and thy choice,
Who madest him thy chosen, that he seem'd
To his great heart none other than a God!
I ask'd thee, "Give me immortality."                          15
Then didst thou grant mine asking with a smile,
Like wealthy men who care not how they give.
But thy strong Hours indignant work'd their wills,
And beat me down and marr'd and wasted me,
And tho' they could not end me, left me maim'd         20
To dwell in presence of immortal youth,
Immortal age beside immortal youth,
And all I was, in ashes. Can thy love,
Thy beauty, make amends, tho' even now,
Close over us, the silver star, thy guide,                     25
Shines in those tremulous eyes that fill with tears
To hear me? Let me go: take back thy gift:
Why should a man desire in any way
To vary from the kindly race of men,
Or pass beyond the goal of ordinance                         30
Where all should pause, as is most meet for all?
A soft air fans the cloud apart; there comes
A glimpse of that dark world where I was born.
Once more the old mysterious glimmer steals
From thy pure brows, and from thy shoulders pure,    35
And bosom beating with a heart renew'd.
Thy cheek begins to redden thro' the gloom,
Thy sweet eyes brighten slowly close to mine,
Ere yet they blind the stars, and the wild team
Which love thee, yearning for thy yoke, arise,            40
And shake the darkness from their loosen'd manes,
And beat the twilight into flakes of fire.
Lo! ever thus thou growest beautiful

47

In silence, then before thine answer given
Departest, and thy tears are on my cheek.                   45
    Why wilt thou ever scare me with thy tears,
And make me tremble lest a saying learnt,
In days far-off, on that dark earth, be true?
"The Gods themselves cannot recall their gifts."
    Ay me! ay me! with what another heart                   50
In days far-off, and with what other eyes
I used to watch—if I be he that watch'd—
The lucid outline forming round thee; saw
The dim curls kindle into sunny rings;
Changed with thy mystic change, and felt my blood          55
Glow with the glow that slowly crimson'd all
Thy presence and thy portals, while I lay,
Mouth, forehead, eyelids, growing dewy-warm
With kisses balmier than half-opening buds
Of April, and could hear the lips that kiss'd              60
Whispering I knew not what of wild and sweet,
Like that strange song I heard Apollo sing,
While Ilion like a mist rose into towers.
    Yet hold me not for ever in thine East:
How can my nature longer mix with thine?                   65
Coldly thy rosy shadows bathe me, cold
Are all thy lights, and cold my wrinkled feet
Upon thy glimmering thresholds, when the steam
Floats up from those dim fields about the homes
Of happy men that have the power to die,                   70
And grassy barrows of the happier dead.
Release me, and restore me to the ground.
Thou seëst all things, thou wilt see my grave;
Thou wilt renew thy beauty morn by morn;
I earth in earth forget these empty courts,                75
And thee returning on thy silver wheels.

The poem begins with four lines of lyrical lament that appear
to bewail earthly mortality: the woods decay, man dies, the swan
dies. But lines 5–6 bring a surprise: Tithonus envies the mortal
nature of human life: "Me only cruel immortality /
Consumes," he complains, and the shock of this statement is increased considerably by the placing of the verb at the end and the object at
the beginning of the sentence. The oxymoron "cruel immortality" also produces a certain surprise. Lines 6–10 begin to give us
some context: the words "I wither" and "white-hair'd shadow"

indicate Tithonus' age; the expression "thine arms" shows that he is addressing an auditor—who, for any reader who knows the myth, must be Eos, as the references to "the East" and "morn" confirm. These lines also give some indication of place: "Here at the quiet limit of the world," in "The ever-silent spaces of the East"—the realm of the dawn.

In line 15 we learn that Tithonus asked Eos for immortal life; Tennyson has altered the myth somewhat here, since in Homer it was Eos who asked Zeus. No doubt Tennyson wanted to give Eos more power over Tithonus: the whole poem consists of his plea to her to retract the gift of immortality. Also, the poem suggests that Tithonus is being punished for his pride in making such a request: the reason he gives for having made it is not that he wished to continue loving Eos for her own sake, but that his pride in being her lover caused him to desire godhead for himself (ll. 13–14). Now he has learned humility and the wisdom of being content with normal human existence and "the goal of ordinance"—a normal life span (ll. 28–31); however, it is too late—he is immortal. He pleads with Eos to take back her gift (ll. 27, 72), but she does not answer. Her whole attitude is ambiguous: is her smile of line 16 simply a generous response to his request, or a malicious smile because she realized that he would grow old? When Tithonus claims that her eyes fill with tears at hearing his lament (ll. 26–27), should we go along with his interpretation of these tears as an expression of sympathy, or should we remember that the dawn, as a natural phenomenon, is always accompanied by dew, so that the presence of "tears," here and in line 45, may have no reference to Tithonus and his plight?

Dawn's failure to respond to Tithonus can be interpreted in different ways. The poem conveys the impression that Tithonus is not making his request for the first time (cf. ll. 43–46) or for the last, but that he repeats it daily. Why does she not reply? Daniel Harris suggests that, as a goddess, she does not even comprehend human speech;[15] yet she certainly understood his initial request for immortality, according to the poem (ll. 15–16), and granted it. Apparently, then, she understands Tithonus, though she may not have the capacity for human speech. Certainly she is characterized in the poem by her silence: "Lo! ever thus thou growest beautiful / In silence" (cf. also ll. 7, 9). Of course, as the auditor of a dramatic monologue she is prevented from speaking by the formal properties of the genre; so that the form Tennyson has chosen for his poem enhances its effect. Another result of this silence is to suggest the theme of divine indifference—one that crops up from time to time in Tennyson's works, for example in "The Lotos-Eaters."

Tithonus is afraid that Eos does not respond to his pleas because, so he has heard, "The Gods themselves cannot recall their gifts" (l. 49)—in which case he is trapped forever in eternal decrepitude. No doubt the pun here on the word "recall" is deliberate. They may not retract their gifts, or they may not *remember* them: memory depends on Time, which may have no meaning for immortal gods. And so Tithonus would continue forever his daily lamentation, summoning up images of the dawn's beauty, pleading with Eos to release him, and bemoaning his own "withered immortality."[16] As in Browning's monologue "Andrea del Sarto," one has the impression, reading Tithonus' speech, that he has said it all before and will say it again.

A large proportion of the poem is taken up with enchanting descriptions of the dawn, both as Tithonus witnesses it now (ll. 32–42), and as he remembers himself loving Eos in days gone by (ll. 50–63)—though with the words "if I be he that watch'd" (l. 52), he distances himself from that former self, which now seems so far away. His use of the third person with reference to himself in lines 11–14 also suggests alienation from his past self. As well as conveying his passionate yearning, his descriptions of the dawn are particularly effective in suggesting both a natural phenomenon and the anthropomorphic features of a goddess: "Thy cheek begins to redden thro' the gloom" (l. 37) evokes both a human blush and a reddening of the sky at dawn; "I used to watch . . . / the lucid outline forming round thee; saw / The dim curls kindle into sunny rings" (l. 52–54) is suggestive of both real curls and of the bright outline around clouds.

The stress Tithonus lays on Dawn's beauty throughout the poem leads the reader to wonder about the wholeheartedness of his desire for release from immortality. In the last paragraph of the poem Tithonus reiterates his request for release; the apparent contradictions of lines 70–71 ("happy men that have the power to die" and "the happier dead") reveal the extent of Tithonus' weariness with his overextended life. He looks forward to a time when, if he is released, he will be "earth in earth" and able to forget Eos; nevertheless, the last line of the poem evokes again her beauty and her daily renewal. One senses that what he would really like is a permanent return to the days of his youth. The poem represents, as W. David Shaw suggests, a Keatsian "quest for both permanence and immediacy," questioning whether it is "ever possible for the beauty and nobility in life to triumph over time."[17]

Unlike a Keatsian ode, however, "Tithonus," being a dramatic monologue, has a certain narrative dimension. Though it does not retell Tithonus' story, it relies on the reader's knowledge of that story. Indeed, "Tithonus" is clearly a dramatic monologue, with a speaker identified as Other by his name and situation, and placed in a specific setting, in circumstances that certainly qualify as dramatic, involving as they do decisions about life and death. Yet how different this poem is from "The Bishop Orders His Tomb" and other dramatic monologues by Browning. The Bishop is located in a precise historical and spatial context—in Rome, on his deathbed, in the 16th century—and he refers to realistic, concrete aspects of everyday life, such as his bath, precious stones, his church, tombstone, and so on. Tithonus, a mythical figure, resides outside Time, in eternity, "at the quiet limit of the world." Indications of time and place are extremely vague and not at all realistic. The "ever-silent spaces of the East" belong to the mythical world of the goddess of the dawn. Whereas Browning creates a fictional world imitating reality—as in a novel—and pinpoints his characters in a specific setting, Tennyson prefers, on the whole, the world of myth. Time and place are of far less importance in myths because the latter have a universal quality, often illustrating some general aspect of human behavior—in Tithonus' case, excessive pride or ambition. Characterization also becomes irrelevant: Tithonus stands, in a sense, for man in general, and we need to know very little about him as a person; whereas the Bishop has a definite personality of his own and illustrates the vices of a particular era.

The split that inevitably occurs in a dramatic monologue between the voice of the speaker and that of the poet is more marked in Browning's monologues than in Tennyson's. As readers, we hear an ironic discrepancy between the Bishop's assessment of himself and the view suggested by the poet's manipulation of language and mention of significant details. This ironic strategy is common in Browning's poems, but judgments of

Tennyson's protagonists are harder to make because he is less inclined to choose reprehensible characters, or indeed to endow his speakers with recognizable personality at all. Hughes draws a distinction between the monologues of Browning and Tennyson based on their concern with personality or with consciousness, respectively. The stress on personality that we find in Browning's work leads to an outward "orientation of the human agent to the world and others," whereas Tennyson's concern with consciousness produces a more inward-looking movement (Hughes, 1987, 14–15). Thus we see the Bishop of Saint Praxed in his relations with the ecclesiastical world around him, and in conflict with his sons, whereas "Tithonus" is more concerned with the inner struggle that leads the speaker to request death in spite of his continuing love for Eos.

Harris, noting the split in the language of dramatic monologues ("the speech of these poems is spoken doubly, from two sources simultaneously, but not with consonant meanings") sees the divergence in "Tithonus" as resulting from the speaker's personification of the dawn, which produces "tension between Tithonus' attitude towards the Dawn (she is a divinity) and Tennyson's (the dawn is a phenomenon that the protagonist has personified)" (Harris, 16 and 13). Tithonus is endowed with even less character than Ulysses. At most he illustrates, in the way of myths, one facet of human nature in general: hubris, or overweening pride. The reader may hesitate between two reactions to his plight: sympathy when he appeals to Eos for release, and ridicule, inevitably evoked by the idea of an old man with "wrinkled feet" desiring the embrace of a young and beautiful woman. His admission that he sought immortality not out of love for Eos but because he "seem'd / To his great heart none other than a God!" also condemns him, though he does show regret for this earlier pride (ll. 28–31) and a desire to belong once again to "the kindly race of men"; yet the reader senses that his real longing is for the days of his youth when, he says, he was "glorious in his beauty and thy choice" (l. 12).

The differences between Browning's and Tennyson's dramatic monologues in the realm of setting and characterization are accompanied by linguistic differences. Commenting on their widely diverging treatments of the dramatic monologue, Herbert F. Tucker suggests that, with poems such as "Ulysses" and "Tithonus," Tennyson "in effect re-lyricized the genre, running its contextualizing devices in reverse and stripping his speakers of personality in order to facilitate a lyric drive" (Tucker, 229). It seems awkward to speak of re-lyricizing a genre that had yet to be established as a genre in 1833, when "Ulysses" and "Tithon" were composed; but certainly Tennyson's impulse is toward lyricism, whereas Browning concentrates more on dramatic incident, narrative, and character. The language of Browning's protagonists helps to define them. A speaker like the Bishop has his own idiosyncratic style, with a vocabulary specific to him, and with the intonations, rhythms, and syntax of spoken, even colloquial, language. Tithonus, in contrast, speaks as befits a representative of mankind as a whole, in a much more noble, conventionally poetic tone. His diction is not colloquial, he does not interrupt himself, express hesitation, digress, or leave sentences unfinished, as does the Bishop. If he employs exclamations, he places them at the beginning of sentences ("Alas! for this gray shadow . . . ."; "Ay me! ay me! with what another heart . . . ."), rather than interrupting his own thought as the Bishop does ("Nephews—sons mine . . . ah God, I know not! Well—"). And far from indulging in the loose, disjointed syntax of conversation, Tithonus produces highly structured sentences with some elegant inversions like the one in lines 5–6, or other latinate constructions such as "before thine answer given" or "thy strong Hours indignant work'd their wills." Such syntax is typical of Tennyson, both in dramatic monologues and in his other poetry. He also often employs circumlocutions (impressive-sounding ways of expressing something rather simple) as when he describes King Arthur's mustache in "The Passing of Arthur" as "a knightly growth that fringed his lips." Walter Bagehot objected to Tennyson's "ornate" style, which can at times be irritating, but also enriching when successful.[18]

Nevertheless, "Tithonus" shares certain linguistic characteristics with most dramatic monologues, including Browning's. Because dramatic monologues are almost always addressed to an interlocutor, their language usually possesses some features of dialogue: the poem is addressed to a "you" (or a "thou") who represents the auditor (even when, as in soliloquies, the auditor is the other half of the speaker's self); and as in dialogue, questions and imperatives abound. Tithonus addresses Eos as "thou"; he asks her several questions, as in lines 23–27, 28–31 (though this question may be addressed to himself), 46–48, and 65. He also uses imperatives: "Let me go; take back thy gift"; "hold me not for ever in thine East:" "Release me, and restore me to the ground."[19] Like other dramatic monologues, "Tithonus" also contains several deictics, expressions which imply presence in a specific setting. When Tithonus says "Here" in line 7, the word places him in a certain space (even if only "the quiet limit of the world"!)—as again, in line 75, when he refers to "*these* empty courts." Similarly, the phrase "even now" (l. 24) indicates that he actually sees, at the moment of speech, the "silver star" (Venus) that announces the dawn. Thus the dramatic monologue produces a feeling of actuality, which reinforces the link between the speaker and his setting. Hughes notes the ironic appropriateness of the dramatic monologue form for a poem about Tithonus, who longs to escape the everlasting present in which he is trapped, to "be part of a third-person past-tense narrative, where he . . . is locked safely away into the past" (Hughes, 100).

Like "The Bishop Orders His Tomb," "Tithonus" is composed in blank verse, in what Elaine Jordan calls "the authoritative tread of the iambic pentameter." Iambic pentameter (a line of five feet, each containing one unstressed syllable followed by a stressed one) is the meter of Shakespeare, as Jordan points out (Jordan, 63–64). Robert Pattison also comments that Tennyson's pentameters perform "one of the traditional functions of English blank verse, the rendering of dramatic speech" (Pattison, 141). But whereas in "The Bishop" the rhythm of the iambic pentameters is frequently and deliberately undermined by run-on lines or pauses within lines for the sake of creating an impression of oral discourse, Tennyson's blank verse knows it is verse. His speakers' utterances sound like poetry, not speech. As well as avoiding colloquialisms and the loose syntax of conversation, "Tithonus" is rhythmically fairly regular, though with variations, as always, on the basic iambic pentameter. There are far fewer examples of pauses in mid-line (ll. 6, 23, 27, 32), and of run-on lines, than in Browning's monologues with their oral bias. One might note the rhythm of line 19 ("And beat me down and marr'd and wasted me"), in which the heavy beat of the monosyllables imitates the action described.

Effects of alliteration, repetition, or rhythm in Browning's monologues usually are aimed at creating dramatic suspense or emphasizing some aspect of character or situation, rather than producing a musical effect. Tennyson, in contrast, with his liking for mellifluous verse, values such poetic effects for their own sake or for the creation of mood. A line like "The long day wanes; the slow moon climbs; the deep / Moans round with many voices" (from "Ulysses"), with its pauses, long slow vowel sounds, and alliteration of *l*, *m*, and *n*, creates a melancholy atmosphere in a way that is typical of Tennyson.

The repetitions in the first two lines of "Tithonus" reflect the cyclical nature of the phenomenon of decay but also, with their *w* and vowel sounds, set up the unhappy tone of the poem. Other noticeable repetitions of words come in lines 21–22 when Tithonus characterizes himself and Eos as abstractions—immortal age and immortal youth: opposites who should not be together, as the end of the poem again emphasizes by repetition ("morn by morn" for Eos, "earth in earth" for Tithonus). The word "ashes" in line 23 harks back to "Consumes" in line 6 in a possible reminiscence of Shakespeare's Sonnet 73: " . . . the glowing of such fire, / That on the ashes of his youth doth lie / . . . / Consum'd with that which it was nourish'd by." The repeated word "pure" in line 35 ("From thy pure brows, and from thy shoulders pure") calls attention to this aspect of Eos's—and the dawn's—beauty, thanks especially to the positioning of the adjective after the second noun and thus at the end of the line. The "rosy shadows" of the dawn (l. 66) recall Tithonus' reference to himself as a "gray shadow" in line 11. Amazingly, these warm-sounding "rosy shadows" bathe Tithonus "Coldly" (l. 66), an effect Tennyson maintains by repeating "cold" twice more in this line and the next, and that contrasts strongly with the heat engendered in lines 55–56: " . . . and felt my blood / Glow with the glow that slowly crimson'd all." The same *o* sound that evokes an inviting warmth when accompanied by *l* in these lines ("blood . . . Glow . . . glow . . . slowly . . . all") returns in the later line (66) with consonants *k* and *d* to suggest cold and indifference ("Coldly . . . rosy shadows . . . cold").

Alliteration and assonance are essential to Tennyson's poetry; their effects are hard to analyze, and the reader is not always conscious of them. A good example in "Tithonus" is line 9, "The ever-silent spaces of the East," where the repetition of *s* evokes this silence. Silence, and the sound *s*, are associated with Eos throughout the rest of the poem, for example, in lines 25–26: "Close over us, the silver star, thy guide, / Shines in those tremulous eyes that fill with tears," or lines 43–44: "Lo! ever thus thou growest beautiful / In silence." The last line of the poem, "And thee returning on thy silver wheels" (recalling the "silver star" of line 25), again suggests silence, therefore, without even mentioning the word. Dawn is also associated, appropriately enough, with light: "gleaming halls," "silver star," "mysterious glimmer," "sweet eyes brighten," "flakes of fire," "lucid outline," "sunny rings," "Glow," "lights," "glimmering thresholds," and so on.

The passage describing the dawn (ll. 32–42) contains many alliterative effects (such as the *f* in "A soft air fans," the thump of the *b* in "bosom beating with a heart renew'd," or the strenuous longing evoked by the initial *y* sounds in "yearning for thy yoke"), culminating in the wonderful line, "And beat the twilight into flakes of fire." The image "flakes of fire," with its connotations of flames and snowflakes, vividly suggests the bright rays of dawn emerging out of the gray twilight—as well as conveying the fire of Tithonus' passion for Eos. The image is reinforced by the alliteration of *f* and of the *k*, which refers back to "shake the darkness" in the previous line, where "shake" rhymes internally with "flakes." The verb "beat" in line 42 conveys perfectly the energy of the horses' action, and there is a vigorous and appropriate alliteration of the *t* sound in "beat the twilight into . . . ." Lines like this one substantiate Alan Sinfield's claim that, in Tennyson's poetry, "any particular word has, or appears to have, many reasons for being appropriate: it is linked to other words through effects of sound and rhythm, syntactical parallelism, and figurative associations which may extend through a network of images across hundreds of lines." Such statements point up the resemblances between Tennyson and Symbolist poetry, particularly that of Mallarmé, especially when Sinfield adds that all these effects work "in relative independence of reference to the world: significance begins to seem a property of the poem, not of the world."[20]

Browning's dramatic monologues, on the contrary, are totally bound up in the world, and his aim of reproducing oral speech in poetry precludes the creation of poetic effects for their own sake, since people do not normally speak "poetically." In the mouth of a mythical character like Ulysses or Tithonus, however, poetical diction does not seem as out of place as it would coming from the Bishop of Saint Praxed's.

Tennyson has been accused of overdoing his sound effects; yet when he is successful, as in "Tithonus," the resulting poetic achievement enchants the reader. Indeed, to some, a line like "And beat the twilight into flakes of fire" may seem worth a whole monologue of oral discourse. Tennyson is, first and foremost, a "superb artist in words, a maker of golden lines."[21]

## Other Victorian Poets

Tennyson and Browning published dramatic monologues in their poetry collections of the 1830s and 1840s, but it was not until the publication in 1855 of Tennyson's *Maud* and Browning's *Men and Women* that dramatic monologues came to be written in great numbers. The second half of the 19th century saw a veritable spate of dramatic monologues, composed by well-known poets such as William Morris, George Meredith, Arthur Clough, Dante Gabriel Rossetti and Christina Rossetti, Algernon Swinburne, Rudyard Kipling, and Thomas Hardy. A host of minor poets also contributed to the genre.[22] There is not space here to study any of these poems in detail, but it seems appropriate to look at a few examples from this age of the great flowering of the dramatic monologue form.

Some of William Morris's early poetry of the 1850s and 1860s includes dramatic monologues such as "Riding Together," "Concerning Geffray Teste Noire" and "The Judgment of God"— all very long poems.

Swinburne's "The Leper" appeared in his *Poems and Ballads* of 1866. It is quite a long poem—thirty-five stanzas of four lines each. The speaker is the servant of a noble lady who has contracted leprosy. Swinburne gives his source for the poem as the *Grandes Chroniques de France* (1505) and quotes, in French, the passage from the *Chroniques* relative to the lady in question, Yolande de Sallières. The lady had been very beautiful and much admired, but when she became a leper neither her family nor her former admirers would have anything to do with her. Only her former servant, who was also in love with her, remained with her, and eventually contracted the disease himself. The poem gives the speaker's imagined words after his beloved's death from leprosy, a death that allows him now to touch and kiss her (a necrophilic gesture reminiscent of Browning's "Porphyria's Lover"):

> Yet am I glad to have her dead
> Here in this wretched wattled house
> Where I can kiss her eyes and head.

We see the deictics ("Here," "this") typical of the dramatic monologue, establishing the speaker's presence in a particular environment. The speaker is identified, not by name, but by his status as a leper and a servant. His character is not analyzed, the poem's interest lying more in his dramatic situation. He remembers that in former days, when his lady was beautiful, one of his tasks was to arrange meetings with her lover, who, once she became ill with leprosy, "Found her a plague to turn away." Nevertheless, the lady always remembered that man with regret and could not love the speaker, in spite of his devotion to her even in her diseased state.

Apart from one or two stilted inversions ("But that new shame could make love new / She saw not—yet her shame did make"), the language of this poem generally has the cadences of speech; there are many run-on lines, following the natural syntax of the sentence rather than the verse pattern:

> I never should have kissed her. See
> What fools God's anger makes of men!

The poem contains none of the colloquialisms, nor the hesitations and interruptions we associate with the speech of Browning's protagonists; yet the diction is more natural and the syntax more straightforward than in most of Tennyson's dramatic monologues.

Christina Rossetti's "Maggie a Lady" (1862) also treats the theme of unfulfilled love, though in less morbid circumstances. The speaker, Maggie, is now Lady of the Manor, having risen considerably in the social scale, through her marriage, since the days when she used to play with Philip, whom she addresses in the poem. She is very proud of her newfound elegance and status ("Look at my gown, Philip, and look at my ring"), and very vain ("Am I so fair, Philip? . . . If I was fair then sure I'm fairer now"). She looks down on Philip who is "but a sailor . . . weatherbeaten brown," yet she hints at the end that she still has great affection for him and has essentially given up love for the sake of status—a very Tennysonian theme, though Tennyson, in *Maud* and "Locksley Hall," treats it from the man's point of view. "I'm a great lady in a sheltered bower," declares Maggie, " . . . Yet sometimes I think of you hour after hour / Till I nigh wish myself a child with you."

The syntax of the poem generally is straightforward, and there are questions, exclamations, and commands to the auditor ("Look at my gown, Philip") and run-on lines, all of which help to create an impression of speech. Sometimes, however, the lilting rhythm of the verse contradicts this impression, as in the first stanza:

> You must not call me Maggie, you must not call me Dear,
> For I'm Lady of the manor now stately to see;
> And if there comes a babe, as there may some happy year,
> 'Twill be little lord or lady at my knee.

The tension between the rhythm of poetry and that of speech is a feature of any dramatic monologue that attempts to convey a spoken quality. This tension is very evident in this poem; more subtle in "The Leper," with its shorter, more prosaic lines; and subtler still in Browning's blank verse.

In "Martin's Puzzle," also published in 1862, Meredith uses the dramatic monologue to explore the age-old dilemma of the religious man seeking an explanation for the suffering of the young and innocent. Martin sees Molly go by with a smile on her face and a song on her lips; she has suffered greatly, has lost a leg, and yet seems to bear no resentment. By using the dramatic monologue, Meredith is able to give this abstract problem a concrete context, that of Molly as seen by Martin, a cobbler. Some Browningesque interruptions and interpolations help to create the impression of Martin's speech:

> First, a fool of a boy ran her down with a cart.
> Then, her fool of a father—a blacksmith by trade—
> Why the deuce does he tell us it half broke his heart?
> His heart!—where's the leg of the poor little maid!
> Well that's not enough; they must push her downstairs,
> To make her go crooked . . . .

However, Meredith does not avoid sentimentality ("She sings little hymns at the close of the day, / Though she has but three fingers to lift to the Lord, / And only one leg to kneel down with to pray"); and Martin's conversion at the end of the poem comes out of the blue: "They tell us that discord, though discord, alone, / Can be harmony when the notes properly fit: / Am I judging all things from a single false tone? / . . . I might try at kneeling with Molly tonight."

A later poem, Thomas Hardy's "My Cicely," published in the *Wessex Poems* of 1898, has a date ("17—") as subtitle, like many of Browning's poems. The speaker is not identified by name but only as Cicely's former admirer. He is placed initially in the context of city life, with its "frenzy-led factions" and "Baals illusive and specious," though much of the poem concerns his subsequent journey into the countryside of his youth. He states that he had heard, with grief, that his former beloved, Cicely, had died; but later discovered that this news actually concerned some other Cicely, and that his beloved was still alive—as the first line of the poem dramatically proclaims:

> "Alive?"—And I leapt in my wonder,
>     Was faint of my joyance,
> And grasses and grove shone in garments
>     Of glory to me.

The strong alliteration in these lines helps to convey the speaker's delight at the news. His earlier love rekindled, he sets off from the city to find his Cicely in the country where he had left her, only to learn that she is married to a former servant and was pregnant before marriage:

> "She wedded."—"Ah!"—"Wedded beneath her—
>     She keeps the stage-hostel
> Ten miles hence . . . .
> . . . . . . . . . . . . . . . . . . . . . . . . . . . . . . . . .
> "Her spouse was her lackey—no option
>     'Twixt wedlock and worse things;
> A lapse over-sad for a lady
>     Of her pedigree!"

This news is another shock to the speaker ("More ghastly than death were these tidings / Of life's irony"), for he had stopped at the stage-hostel in question on his way, and had therefore seen Cicely without recognizing her, because of the transformations wrought by her life in the tavern:

> I'd looked on, unknowing, and witnessed
> Her jests with the tapsters,
> Her liquor-fired face, her thick accents
> In naming her fee.

This vision of his former love is so horrible that he has persuaded himself that the real Cicely was in fact the one whose death he originally heard about. For this people call him "Frail-witted," but he does not mind: "Far better / To dream than to own the debasement / Of sweet Cicely."

The short lines of the poem occasionally cause some awkward juxtapositions of words ("frenzy-led factions," "death-rumour") and lines that are hard to pronounce ("Triple-ramparted Maidon gloomed grayly"). But the strong rhythm of the lines gives the poem a distinct forward movement, accentuated by the rhyme (only the last lines of each stanza rhyme with one another, on the *ee* sound). The many examples of alliteration (for example, "A last lullaby," "A cruel decree!" and "From blackbird and bee,") contribute to this forward movement—as does the dramatic, even melodramatic, nature of the story.

Hardy's *Wessex Poems* also includes the dramatic monologue "Valenciennes" spoken by Corporal Tullidge from Hardy's own novel, *The Trumpet-Major;* and some poems spoken by women, such as the four poems entitled "She, to him" and one entitled simply "She," in which a sweetheart, at the funeral of her beloved, complains that she cannot legitimately express her grief, as his family can, even though it "consumes like fire."

A.E. Housman's *A Shropshire Lad* (1896) also contains some dramatic monologues, such as "The Carpenter's Son," in which a young man about to be hanged wishes he had stayed at home and applied himself to his father's trade. "Is My Team Ploughing?" is another dramatic poem—in the form of a dialogue between a dead man and his best friend, who has become the lover of his dead friend's former sweetheart; but one could read the poem as a monologue, with the dead man's words representing the prickings of the live youth's guilty conscience.

In an altogether different vein is the poetry of Rudyard Kipling, whose works include large numbers of dramatic monologues. An example is "McAndrew's Hymn" (1893), spoken by the Scot McAndrew, a ship's engineer, and addressed, as the title suggests, to God. The poem has very long, strongly accented lines, rhymed; and it is written in a highly colloquial style, with Scottish dialect words and pronunciations. Other dramatic monologues by Kipling are "Mulholland's Contract" and "The 'Mary Gloster.'" Kipling achieved the height of fame toward the turn of the century, after which his popularity declined rapidly. He died in oblivion in 1936.

With Hardy, Kipling, and A.E. Housman we come into the twentieth century, and the age of Modernism. Of the great poets of this age—Stevens, Yeats, Pound, and Eliot—the latter two wrote dramatic monologues, some of which we will examine in the next chapter.

# Chapter 3

# THE AGE OF MODERNISM

F our great poets stand out in the Modernist period: W.B. Yeats, T.S. Eliot, Ezra Pound, and Wallace Stevens. Of these, Eliot and Pound both wrote several dramatic monologues in the early stages of their careers, moving on, for the most part, to other forms later. They reacted, inevitably, in varying degrees, to the poetry of their predecessors. Despite an essentially anti-Victorian stance, they both adopted personae, as had Browning and Tennyson, as a means of distancing the poem from the poet; and they both came to admire Browning for his use of the language of speech in poetry.

## Ezra Pound

Pound was born in the United States in 1885 but went to Europe in 1908 and stayed there for most of his life, living first in London, then in France and Italy, where he died in 1972. Immediately after World War II he spent twelve years in a hospital in Washington, D.C., having been indicted for treason but found unfit to stand trial on grounds of insanity. When the indictment was dismissed in 1958 and he was released from hospital, he returned to Italy.

Pound studied Romance Languages at college and was particularly interested in the literature of Provence. He traveled in Provence, as well as Spain and Italy, before going to live in London. His knowledge of Provençal literature is reflected in much of his early poetry and heralds the interest he was later to develop in the Noh plays of Japan, in Chinese poetry, and other foreign literatures. He was also steeped in recent British poetry: Tennyson and Browning, Swinburne and the Rossettis, and the so-called decadents of the nineties—Dowson, Symons, Fiona MacLeod. The latter poets are no longer read so much nowadays but were very popular at the time and imparted to poetry an atmosphere of mystery or dream; imagery of winds, roses, twilights and still pools; and a preference for Celtic scenes. The young Yeats was a leading figure in this movement, though his later poetry developed beyond it.

Pound, who had already started writing when he came to London, soon grew impatient with this kind of poetry, but there are many traces of it in his early work, such as the beginning lines of "Threnos," spoken by Tristan and Isolde:

> No more for us the little sighing.
> No more the winds at twilight trouble us.
>
> Lo the fair dead!
>
> No more do I burn.
> No more for us the fluttering of wings
> That whirred in the air above us.
>
> Lo the fair dead!

or, again, the beginning of "De Aegypto":

> I, even I, am he who knoweth the roads
> Through the sky, and the wind thereof is my body.
>
> I have beheld the Lady of Life,
> I, even I, who fly with the swallows.
>
> Green and gray is her raiment,
> Trailing along the wind.

Both these poems appear in the volume entitled *Personae*, published in London in 1909, and containing, as its title might imply, several dramatic monologues. The word "persona" originally referred to a mask worn by actors in ancient Greek theater to magnify their voices; in modern literary criticism the term refers to the speaker of a poem, whether the speaker is identified, as in a dramatic monologue, or not. In his essay "The Three Voices of Poetry," T.S. Eliot credits Pound with introducing the term, by way of his title, into the modern critical vocabulary "to indicate the historical or fictional mask a poet may assume to address his audience."[1] Other early volumes by Pound are *Ripostes* (1912); *Lustra* (1916); the "Homage to Sextus Propertius" (1919); and *Hugh Selwyn Mauberley*, published in 1920 as a kind of farewell to London when Pound moved to Paris. Thereafter, Pound's poetic output was channeled into *The Cantos*, which he had begun writing in 1915. These are poems of varying length, published at intervals over the years, and of which he was eventually to write over one hundred. Their wide-ranging subject matter includes events from world history and politics as well as literary topics. The work represents a kind of modern epic, and incorporates many voices, though the "I" often clearly represents Pound himself. Michael Bernstein, in *Ezra Pound and the Modern Verse Epic: The Tale of the Tribe*, analyzes Pound's "dilemma of how to use historical figures, how to give speech to others, or . . . to take on others' voices without thereby losing one's own."[2]

The volume *Personae* contains most of the dramatic monologues Pound wrote (though it also includes many poems, such as "De Aegypto," that are not dramatic monologues); and anyone writing dramatic monologues in the early 20th century was bound to look back at the masters of the genre, Browning and Tennyson. Pound felt a great antipathy for Tennyson, largely because he held him partly responsible for a bombastic, patriotic type of poetry that became popular during the Victorian era and was still being written when he arrived in London. He considered that Tennyson's poetic genius had been corrupted by the need, as Poet Laureate, to compose respectable verse to celebrate public events. For Browning, however, he had considerable admiration, contending that his *Men and Women* are the "most interesting poems in Victorian English . . . or, if that statement is too absolute, . . . the form of these poems is the most vital form of

65

that period of English."[3] One of the poems in *Personae* is
addressed to Robert Browning:

> Aye you're a man that! ye old mesmerizer
> Tyin' your meanin' in seventy swadelin's
> One must of needs be a hang'd early riser
> To catch you at worm turning. Holy Odd's bodykins!
> . . . . . . . . . . . . . . . . . . . . . . . . . . . . . . . . . . . . . . . . . . . . .
> You wheeze as a head-cold long-tonsilled Calliope,
> But God! what a sight you ha' got o' our in'ards . . . .

This poem conveys admiration for Browning's knowledge and
understanding of human nature as well as an awareness of the
difficulty of following his meaning at times, and of the unmelo-
dious nature of his verse ("You wheeze . . ."). The title of this
poem, "Mesmerism," gives some indication of the extent of
Browning's influence on Pound; indeed, Pound complained that
he had caught Browning's manner as if it were a disease.[4] Two
elements in particular attracted him to Browning's poetry. One
was his ability to create character ("what a sight you ha' got o'
our in'ards") and to present a story from the point of view of that
character. The other was his use of spoken language, as opposed
to the "stilted language that . . . passed for 'good English'" in
Victorian poetry generally and still in the early 20th century.[5] In a
letter of 1915, Pound recommended avoiding, in poetry, "book
words," periphrases, inversions, clichés, and what he calls
"Tenyssonianness of speech"—or indeed anything "that you
couldn't, in some circumstance, in the stress of some emotion,
actually say." He declared that the language of poetry should
depart "in no way from speech save by heightened intensity,"[6]
and he eventually worked out for himself an original voice
reflecting this conviction. In those poems of *Personae* that use
spoken language, however, the speakers still sound like
Browning's characters. "When we read the early monologue,
'Cino,'" as Thomas H. Jackson says, "there can be no doubt
where Pound went to school. When Cino imagines his women
speaking, they speak Browning's English":[7]

> "Cino?" "Oh, eh, Cino Polnesi
> The singer is't you mean?"
> "Ah yes, passed once our way,
> A saucy fellow, but . . .

(Oh they are all one these vagabonds),
Peste! 'tis his own songs?
Or some other's that he sings?
But *you*, My Lord, how with your city?"

"Cino" is one of several dramatic monologues in *Personae*; yet
Pound felt that Browning had achieved so much with his version
of the dramatic monologue that he himself could only wonder
"What's left for me to do? / Whom shall I conjure up? . . . / Whom
shall I hang my shimmering garment on?" (*Three Cantos*, I, 1915,
later rewritten). These lines reveal Pound's concern with finding
an appropriate persona, as indeed does the title *Personae*. In 1914
he wrote:

> In the "search for oneself," in the search for "sincere self-expression,"
> one gropes, one finds some seeming verity. One says "I am" this,
> that, or the other, and with the words scarcely uttered one ceases to
> be that thing.
> I began this search for the real in a book called *Personae*, casting
> off, as it were, complete masks of the self in each poem.[8]

Like Browning, Pound tends to use historical figures as personae, usually poets and musicians. Pound translated poems by
Provençal and other poets, and these translations also work in a
way as "personae," since Pound is talking in the voice of the
dead poet, having chosen, of course, poems that somehow echo
his own experience. Of the poems in *Personae* that are not translations but dramatic monologues, many enact documented incidents from dead poets' lives; however, his treatment of these
speakers differs in some respects from Browning's. The reference
to "masks of the self" in the above quotation implies that Pound
sees his historical figures as vehicles for self-expression rather
than solely as characters interesting in themselves.

In the first of the *Three Cantos*, Pound says, addressing
Browning, "You had one whole man? / And I have many fragments, less worth?" He feels that Browning could create "one
whole man," but that he has to deal with "many fragments"
because the "beastly and cantankerous age" in which he lives
precludes the portrayal of whole characters. Also, he likes to con-
centrate on a moment of intense experience rather than giving a
complete picture of his protagonist's life: "I catch the character I
happen to be interested in at the moment he interests me, usu-

ally a moment of song, self-analysis, or sudden understanding or revelation." He calls this "the poetic part of a drama the rest of which (to me the prose part) is left to the reader's imagination or implied or set in a short note."[9] (Indeed, several of his dramatic monologues are preceded by a note giving relevant details of the speaker's life.) He is therefore aiming at a type of poem more purely expressive of a mood than Browning's.

A considerable number of poems in *Personae* (for example, "De Aegypto," "La Fraisne," "The Tree," "Praise of Ysolt," "And Thus in Ninevah," "The White Stag," and "Francesca") present a given speaker's "moment of song," with little or no emphasis on story or character. Others resemble Browning's in their portrayal of a particularized individual in specific circumstances, though still concentrating on a certain dramatic moment in the speaker's life. This group includes "La Fraisne," "Cino," "Marvoil," "Sestina: Altaforte," "Na Audiart," "Piere Vidal Old," and the "Ballad of the Goodly Fere." Of these, all but the last are set in Provence and have Provençal poets as speakers.

"Marvoil" presents an incident in the life of a 12th-century Provençal troubadour, Arnaut de Mareuil, whose name Pound anglicizes to "Marvoil." Mareuil's life (like that of many troubadours) was recounted after his death in an anonymous biography (*vida*); it is not necessarily accurate, however, being based largely on the poetry itself, which may not always be autobiographical. In 1896 a collection of such biographies, *The Lives of the Troubadours*, was published in English by Ida Farnell. Mareuil's poetry celebrates his constant love for one woman, unnamed; the *vida* names her as the Countess of Béziers. Pound's "Marvoil" concerns this relationship, though some aspects of the incident recounted in the poem are fictional. Pound did not feel obliged to conform strictly to known facts; his aim was to reproduce the spirit of an age and the possible feelings of a man—a poet—in a particular situation.

Marvoil refers to himself in the first line as "Arnaut the less" because he shared first names with another great Provençal poet, Arnaut Daniel. Pound, borrowing this distinction from Petrarch, who calls Arnaut de Mareuil "'l men famoso Arnaldo" (*Trionfo d'Amore*, IV, l. 44), makes his Marvoil apply the comparison to himself. Mareuil did, apparently, come from a poor family and did work as a clerk, as the first line of the poem suggests, but he preferred to adopt the wandering life of a troubadour, "rambling the South" of France. Pound dramatizes Mareuil's dislike of a clerk's work by stressing his boredom: ". . . I have small mind to sit / Day long, long day cooped on a stool / A-jumbling o' figures for Maître Jacques Polin." The boring nature of the work is emphasized by repetitions of words and sounds in "Day long, long day cooped on a stool." The name of Maître Polin is fictitious, but, because it seems real, adds an air of authenticity.

According to the Provençal *vida*, Mareuil was at the court of Roger II, Viscount of Béziers, and was in love with Roger's wife ("I made rimes to his lady this three year"). The love affair could progress unhindered, the poem suggests, since Roger of Béziers was often away from home ("Beziers off at Mont-Ausier"—the home of another famous Provençal lady, Tibors of Montausier). In a note to the 1909 edition of *Personae*, Pound explains that Tibors was "contemporary with the other persons" in this poem, but admits that he had "no strict warrant for dragging her name into this particular affair." Roger's convenient absences left his lady and Marvoil "Singing the stars in the turrets of Beziers." But Alfonso II of Aragon also loved Roger's wife and was jealous of the affection she showed Mareuil, eventually forcing her to dismiss the troubadour from her service. The end result, according to Marvoil, is: "Aragon cursing in Aragon, Beziers busy at Beziers— / Bored to an inch of extinction"—presumably because he preferred to visit Tibors at Montausier; Tibors herself, who apparently appreciated these visits, is now on her own, "all tongue and temper at Mont-Ausier." As for Marvoil himself, he is exiled to Avignon: "Me! in this damn'd inn of Avignon, / Stringing long verse for the Burlatz." Burlatz is the name of his beloved's family; she was Countess of Burlatz before she married Roger, Viscount of Béziers. Marvoil's resentment against Alfonso of Aragon, the cause of these changes, comes out strongly in the next lines: "All for one half-bald, knock-knee'd king of the Aragonese, / Alfonso, Quattro, poke-nose." Marvoil's anger is emphasized by the harsh *k* and *d* sounds of these two lines, and the sharp pauses and repeated *o* in the second—as well as by the insulting vocabulary. (The Alfonso whom Mareuil knew was actually Alfonso II, not "Quattro," and this substitution may have been the result of an error on Pound's part; or perhaps he felt it was of small consequence anyway, and the sounds of "Quattro" suited him better than "Secundo.")

In the second half of the poem, Marvoil abandons this vituperative note in favor of wistful remembrance of his beloved and regret that he cannot be with her. He also moves from narration of actual events to the question of their expression in literary form. He has a parchment (supposedly the present poem) that he plans to hide in a hole in the wall; then, if it is ever found, people will know more about him than from his poems (*canzoni*); this statement refers to the fact that Mareuil's *canzoni* do not give his mistress's name or any of the details included in the present poem. Marvoil addresses the hole in the wall, hoping it will resonate when the wind blows, and sing "the grace of the Lady of Beziers" like a *jongleur* singing his poems (the poems of troubadours generally were sung). The following three lines, with their repetitions of "hollow" and "fill," express the utter emptiness Marvoil feels away from his lady: "So is my heart hollow when she filleth not mine eyes." The phrase "O hole in the wall here" is repeated three times, which stresses the desolation of being reduced to addressing a hole in the wall as if it were an animate being. This sadness is expressed movingly by the sounds of the lines "When the wind blows sigh thou for my sorrow" and "And though thou sighest my sorrow in the wind." Finally, still addressing the wall, Marvoil emphasizes the need for continued secrecy, "Keep yet my secret in thy breast here": for the sake of his lady's reputation no one must know her name. The final line of the poem, in Latin, simply means "I no longer have the parchment": he has placed it in the wall.

The poems of the troubadour Arnaut de Mareuil tell us little about his personality or his life. For the purposes of his dramatic monologue, Pound has constructed a narrative from a few details of Mareuil's biography, such as his love for the Countess of Béziers and the fact that he left Béziers in 1194. This story is noticeably less complete, however, than those of Browning's dramatic monologues; as Pound himself says, he likes to catch his characters at a particularly significant moment in their lives, "usually a moment of song, self-analysis, or sudden understanding or revelation." In the case of Marvoil, the moment is the enforced departure from Béziers that has deprived him of his happiness. As for his personality, it is also less thoroughly treated than in a Browning poem, but again Pound was not attempting to represent "one whole man" in Marvoil, but his reaction to a particular—and intrinsically dramatic—moment in his life. He has gone so far as to endow Marvoil with characteristics that are not obvious from Mareuil's poetry: anger and resentment at Alfonso of Aragon and an ability to express such feelings very forcefully: "one half-bald, knock-knee'd king of the Aragonese / Alfonso, Quattro, poke-nose." The first half of the poem suggests the speaker's vigor and energy; another side of his character comes out in the second half, which expresses tenderness, regret, and complete fidelity to his lady.

As befits a dramatic monologue, the speaker of "Marvoil" is identified as a persona other than the poet, Pound. Yet by choosing a poet as speaker—as he does in many of his dramatic monologues—Pound implies that he felt a great deal of sympathy with the speaker's viewpoint, and admiration for his poetry; the choice corresponds to Pound's declaration that the protagonists of *Personae* were like a series of "masks of the self."

Marvoil is placed in a particular context: the south of France, and specifically the "damn'd inn of Avignon." The word "jongleur" and the references to historical characters establish the era. Several deictic expressions emphasize the speaker's presence in this setting. He is in "*this* damn'd inn of Avignon," and he has "taken to rambling the South *here*." The deictic word *here* is repeated several times in the second half of the poem, as Marvoil imagines his lady "Close in my arms here" and addresses the "hole in the wall here"; indeed, *here* is the last word of the poem.

The only mention of an interlocutor is the word "friends" at the end of line 15; one can imagine Marvoil addressing other patrons of the inn, probably over a drink. However, he seems to be on his own in the second half of the poem, addressing the hole in the wall and secretly hiding his parchment. The language of this second half consequently has less of the spoken quality of the first.

The diction of Mareuil's poetry in no way resembles the colloquial style of Pound's "Marvoil," a style that clearly owes much to Browning. The opening line, "A poor clerk I, 'Arnaut the less' they call me," recalls the beginning of Browning's "Fra Lippo Lippi": "I am poor brother Lippo, by your leave." The colloquial vocabulary of the poem, especially the insults and imprecations, is reminiscent of many of Browning's monologues with energetic speakers, such as "Fra Lippo Lippi," "The Bishop Orders His Tomb at Saint Praxed's Church," or "Soliloquy of the Spanish Cloister." Marvoil uses the word "damn'd" twice, and invents vigorous epithets for Alfonso: "half-bald," "knock-knee'd," "poke-nose." He shortens words ("A-jumbling o' figures," "I ha' taken"), and his syntax contains some ellipses, as in: "Then came what might come, to wit: three men and one woman, / Beziers off at Mont-Ausier . . . ."; or "Tibors all tongue and temper at Mont-Ausier, / Me! in this damn'd inn of Avignon . . . ." The many run-on lines also convey the rhythm of speech, as in ". . . Alfonso the half-bald, took to hanging / His helmet at Beziers" and "I and his lady / Singing the stars in the turrets of Beziers." It is easier to convey a spoken rhythm in a poem such as this, written in free verse with stanzas of irregular length, than in one with formal rhymed stanzas or even blank verse. Nevertheless, free verse is not prose and is not the same as speech. The variations in rhythm still constitute rhythm, which can be used subtly to convey different emotions, as in the short, choppy, indignant line "Alfonso, Quattro, poke-nose," or the more regular and mellifluous

> O hole in the wall here! be thou my jongleur
> As ne'er had I other, and when the wind blows,
> Sing thou the grace of the Lady of Beziers.

A short line among longer ones can receive an emphasis appropriate to its import, as with the line "Close in my arms here," which conveys Marvoil's longing. Similarly, at the beginning of the fourth stanza, the short line "And if when I am dead" abruptly introduces a new mood.

Pound had studied the free verse of French poets such as Jules Laforgue, and his own use of free verse enhances a trend he admired in Browning, that of allowing poetry to echo the cadences of speech. In his later works, Pound moves away from the direct use of masks and personae, and from the form of the dramatic monologue as such (though the *Cantos* include the voices of a variety of figures, often historical), but his poetry retains the intonations of speech and the rhythms of the human voice.

T.S. Eliot is another modernist poet who appreciated Browning's adoption of a conversational tone in his poetry. Eliot said of Browning that he was the only 19th-century poet "to devise a way of speech which might be useful for others," and that this was achieved largely through his insistence on "the relation of poetry to speech."[10]

## T.S. Eliot

"Despite their anti-Victorianism," says Carol T. Christ, "Modernist poets explore ways of objectifying poetry that show striking continuities with Victorian poetics." One way is to adopt masks and personae, "which, like the Victorian dramatic monologue, distance the poem from the poet"; another is to use "structures of myth and history which provide a narrative that contains and gives significance to personalities."[11] Eliot employs both these strategies. Many of his poems have a mythical dimension, and, at least in the early part of his career, he wrote several dramatic monologues with distinct personae.

As with Pound, however, one can detect in Eliot's poetic works a movement away from his early use of dramatic monologue: from poems like "The Love Song of J. Alfred Prufrock," "Portrait of a Lady," and "Gerontion," via *The Waste Land*, which resembles a collage of dramatic monologues with different speakers, to *Four Quartets*, where the only persona is that of the poet.

Born in 1888, three years after Pound, Eliot also traveled in Europe as a young man and, in 1914, took up residence in England where he lived for the rest of his life, eventually becoming a British citizen. His childhood was spent in St. Louis, where he was born, but the family had strong New England connections and took summer vacations there. Later, Eliot pursued his undergraduate and graduate studies at Harvard. Some of his early poems, such as "Cousin Nancy," "Aunt Helen," "The 'Boston Evening Transcript,'" "Portrait of a Lady," and "The Love Song of J. Alfred Prufrock," reflect this New England social background. As a graduate student, Eliot spent a year in Paris (1910–1911) and then returned to Harvard, but he went back to Europe on a traveling fellowship in 1914. When he came to London at the beginning of World War I, Ezra Pound was already there, and the two poets associated closely until Pound's departure for France. Pound was impressed with Eliot's poetry from the start, encouraged him, made suggestions, and even edited some of his poems, notably *The Waste Land*, which he cut to almost half its original manuscript length. He also helped Eliot publish his work and introduced him to literary figures in London.

In 1915 Eliot met and very soon married an English woman, Vivienne Haigh-Wood. This marriage was to cause much anguish and grief to both parties: they were temperamentally unsuited, there is some suggestion of sexual problems, and Vivienne's health was very poor. She suffered from nervous complaints and from a variety of serious illnesses over the years. Eliot also had health problems from time to time, and he felt obliged, in order to support himself and his wife, to work in a bank, which left him little time for writing. Finally, in 1925, he found more congenial work with the publishing firm of Faber and Gwyer (later Faber and Faber), with whom he remained most of his life. The situation with his wife became so unbearable that in 1933 Eliot left her, not without feelings of guilt. She eventually entered a mental home, where she died in 1947. Eliot was subsequently remarried, in 1957, to Valerie Fletcher, with whom he enjoyed eight years of happiness before his death in 1965.

Meanwhile, in 1927, Eliot had become a member of the Church of England. His adoption of the Anglican Church surprised many readers and friends, but he had always believed strongly in the life of the spirit. His grandfather, William Greenleaf Eliot, had founded the Unitarian Church in St. Louis; his mother revered Eliot's grandfather and was also religious. Eliot's graduate studies at Harvard had been in philosophy, including the exploration of Indian religions. If the process of his conversion was slow and subterranean, his religious convictions remained strong throughout the rest of his life, and are reflected in many of his works, expressing what Peter Ackroyd calls an "unattached religious sensibility—the instinct for belief."[12]

Eliot's poetic output is slight compared to that of Pound (or Tennyson or Browning). Yet his reputation as a poet is extremely high; one critic has affirmed that Eliot "has done more than any other writer to explore and expand the possibilities of 20th-century poetry in English."[13] With the publication of *Prufrock and Other Observations* in 1917 he was heralded as a new voice in English poetry, and *The Waste Land* (1922), though controversial at the time, became one of the most influential poems of the 20th century. His other works include a collection of *Poems* published in 1920, which contains "Gerontion" and several poems written in French; *The Hollow Men* (1925), *Ash-Wednesday* (1930), and the *Ariel Poems,* all of which are just a few pages long; and his masterpiece, *Four Quartets,* published between 1935 and 1942. He also wrote plays, or poetic dramas, of which the most famous are *Murder in the Cathedral* and *The Cocktail Party.* In addition he has published several collections of essays, mostly on literary topics, many of which were originally given as lectures.

The slim volume of Eliot's *Collected Poems* has given birth to a wealth of critical commentary: the number of studies and interpretations of the poet's work is overwhelming. Within the domain of the dramatic monologue, "The Love-Song of J. Alfred Prufrock," much-anthologized, is no doubt the most famous and frequently discussed dramatic monologue of the 20th century. The poems contained in the volume *Prufrock and Other Observations* are, in general, "examples of dramatic virtuosity, conceived in terms of monologue and dialogue, 'scene' and character" (Ackroyd, 79–80). Let us have a brief look at one or two aspects of "Prufrock," before turning to "Portrait of a Lady," which we will discuss in detail.

"The Love-Song of J. Alfred Prufrock" begins "Let us go then, you and I," the speaker being identified by the title, where the name J. Alfred Prufrock clashes so oddly with the notion of a love song. The first line suggests that Prufrock is addressing another person; yet he appears to be alone throughout the poem, imagining himself making the visit mentioned in line 12 ("Let us go and make our visit"), or recalling previous social occasions. The poem is therefore a soliloquy, with the "you and I" of the first line representing perhaps two sides of the same speaker—an interpretation corroborated by Prufrock's later suggestion that one needs to "prepare a face to meet the faces that you meet": he is used to acting different roles in society and showing different sides of his personality according to the occasion. The notion of personality as being fragmented or multiple is present in Eliot as in Pound, whom we saw contrasting his "many fragments" with Browning's "whole man."

Another similarity between Eliot and Pound is their use of spoken language in poetry, for which they have at least one common ancestor in Browning. A glance at these opening lines of "Prufrock" reveals that, although Eliot uses fewer exclamations, interjections, and colloquialisms than do Browning or Pound, and although some of the vocabulary belongs to the written language ("tedious," "insidious"), the rhythm and syntax are those of speech: "Let us go then, you and I . . . . / Oh, do not ask, 'What is it?' / Let us go and make our visit." The neat chime of the rhyme at this point seems to indicate a certain ironic intention behind the words. Irony is a salient feature of Eliot's poetry, as of

Browning's, though it works in a somewhat different way. Whereas a poem by Browning such as "The Bishop Orders His Tomb" produces the sense of an ironic discrepancy between the Bishop's opinion of himself and the reader's assessment, Eliot's dramatic monologues enact speakers who are conscious of their shortcomings: they ridicule their own behavior as well as others'. Prufrock is aware of his own indecisiveness and self-conscious about his appearance:

> And indeed there will be time
> To wonder, 'Do I dare?' and, 'Do I dare?'
> Time to turn back and descend the stair,
> With a bald spot in the middle of my hair.

The young man in "Portrait of a Lady," too, makes fun of himself as well as of the Lady.

The title of this poem, written in 1910–1911 and published in *Prufrock and Other Observations* (1917) relates to the novel, *Portrait of a Lady*, by Henry James (1881), whom Eliot admired. Apparently Eliot told Virginia Woolf in 1920 that he had originally planned to develop in the manner of James.[14] The Lady of his poem would certainly fit very easily into one of James' novels depicting upper-class society. Pound, too, wrote a poem entitled "Portrait d'une femme."

Eliot's poem is divided into three parts: the first takes place in winter (December), the second in spring (April), and the third, when the young man announces his imminent departure abroad, in October—the beginning of another winter, which the lady will sit out "serving tea to friends." This third part ends with a paragraph in which he imagines himself in the future, abroad, reacting with remorse to news of the lady's death. The allusion to death is foreshadowed in the poem's epigraph, taken from Marlowe's *The Jew of Malta:* "Thou hast committed— / Fornication: but that was in another country, / And besides, the wench is dead." These words are much more forceful, dismissive, and definite than the situation in the poem, where the death is imagined, not real; the difference in tone between the terms "wench" and "Lady" is also significant. Furthermore, the accusation ("Fornication") leveled against himself by the Jew in the play is succinct and brutal, whereas in the poem the reasons for the protagonist's culpability in relation to the lady are less clear. His sense of remorse appears to arise more from what he has failed to do than from what he has "committed." He has not responded to her advances, and feels a need to "make a cowardly amends" not for something *he* has done but "For what she has said to me." It seems therefore that the poem represents a highly attenuated version of the situation in the epigraph. From a bald and brutal statement of shocking events—death and fornication—we move to a world where sexual adventures and death are merely envisaged.

The lady, older than the protagonist, is lonely, crying out for love, but he cannot respond; he is desperate to retain his youthful freedom and independence. Because we see the lady through his ironic gaze, we find her behavior embarrassing, her remarks totally predictable, and her transparent attempts to flatter his ego unconvincing, for instance in the passage (lines 24–28) where she hints at her appreciation of his qualities as a friend. Apparently Eliot knew a lady who used to serve tea to students from Harvard in her house on Beacon Hill, and who may well have served as a model for this poem.[15] Also, as we shall see, the poems of the French poet Jules Laforgue, whom Eliot greatly admired in his youth, frequently enact situations where a young man feels ill-at-ease in his relations with a woman.

The setting at the beginning of the poem is deliberately intimate, shutting out the smoke and fog, lit only by candles. But the young man subverts this evocation of a cozy tête-à-tête and exposes its false, theatrical nature by calling it "An atmosphere of Juliet's tomb." The lady may see herself in the role of Juliet, but he is no Romeo; he remembers that *that* love-story ends in death, as he will later imagine the lady's death. He mocks the deliberate stage-setting—"You have the scene arrange itself . . . ." It is not clear whether the "You" here means "one," or refers to himself, or, most likely, since she is the manipulator of scenes, to the lady, whom he would therefore be addressing here in the second person, though he does not do so again in the poem, referring to her only as "she."

The social context is that of the cultured upper class, going to concerts, for example ("let us say") "to hear the latest Pole / Transmit the Preludes, through his hair and finger-tips." Even the pianist seeks to create a deliberate effect by shaking his hair as he plays. The lady moves from the topic of the concert to that of friendship by way of the suggestion that Chopin should be played only to an audience of two or three (preferably two, no doubt) "who will not touch the bloom / That is rubbed and questioned in the concert room." The artificial posturing of this remark grates on the young man's nerves, as does her subsequent flattery of him, giving him a headache ("Inside my brain a dull tom-tom begins") and a longing to escape. This grating sensation is conveyed by the affected use of a foreign word (*cauchemar*, a nightmare), by the break in rhythm of the line "'Without these friendships—life, what *cauchemar!*'", and by harsh consonant sounds: "And the ariettes / Of cracked cornets . . . ." The musical theme initiated by the concert continues in the references to musical instruments, becoming very unmusical with "the ariettes / Of cracked cornets" and the drumbeat in his brain. The "'false note'" associated with this music echoes the falsity of the relationship between the lady and the young man.

As a refuge from the unwanted feminine charms of the lady, the young man envisages a series of more masculine activities: taking the air "in a tobacco trance," admiring monuments, discussing current events, and drinking in a bar.

He returns in April (and may have been back between these visits, we do not know); it is spring, so the lady has lilac blossom in her room. Adopting the pose of experienced older woman, she bemoans the cruelty of youth, which "smiles at situations which it cannot see." The young man, at a loss for words, dutifully smiles, appearing thereby to reinforce the truth of her remark, though in fact he can see through *this* situation very clearly and is determined not to be caught in her net.

The lady is affected by the spring, which reminds her of "Paris in the Spring" and her "buried life." This last phrase refers to a poem by Matthew Arnold whose title, "The Buried Life," designates the life of the emotions, of love and affection. The lady would like nothing better than to give herself up to such emotions; moved by the promptings of spring, she says as much as she dares to the young man without making an open declaration of love: "'I am always sure that you understand / My feelings, always sure that you feel, / Sure that across the gulf you reach your hand.'" This is patently untrue, which is why her voice resembles "the insistent out-of-tune / Of a broken violin." She is playing a part, the part of "one about to reach her journey's end," she says, but also of one who, by such a statement, calls out for sympathy without appearing to do so. She claims that her role is to "'sit here, serving tea to friends,'" but this is clearly a ploy to win his sympathy; there is another role that she would prefer . . . . The young man, too, is aware of playing a part, both when he is with the lady, smiling enigmatically over his teacup, and when he acts the "man about town," discussing the late events or sitting in the park with the newspapers. Like Prufrock, he prepares "a face to meet the faces that you meet."

One stanza in particular of Arnold's poem relates to this theme of social role-playing:

> I knew the mass of men concealed
> Their thoughts, for fear that if revealed
> They would by other men be met
> With blank indifference, or with blame reproved;
> I knew they lived and moved
> Tricked in disguises, alien to the rest
> Of men, and alien to themselves—and yet
> The same heart beats in every human breast!

"Tricked in disguises," "alien to themselves"—these phrases are very relevant to Prufrock and the protagonist of "Portrait of a Lady." The latter may have the upper hand in the complex game that they are playing, but he seems constantly afraid that he might lose that advantage; she obviously exerts some kind of fascination that draws him to her at the risk of losing the independence he values so highly. He puts on an air of ironic indifference, but at times this pose is exposed, for example, when he feels "like one who smiles, and turning shall remark / Suddenly, his expression in a glass." Then his "self-possession gutters." Concerning his "man-about-town" image he claims "I keep my countenance, / I remain self-possessed," but the very fact of making this statement implies that it is not true. He is too self-conscious to be self-possessed, and his self-image never remains the same for long, for he "must borrow every changing shape / To find expression." The "shapes" he mentions are those of wild animals—bear, parrot, and ape; but the bear is a "dancing bear"—it has been tamed and trained to do what does not come naturally; parrots too can be trained to "speak"—to reproduce speech that is meaningless to them; and someone who "apes" other people is playing a role. All these animals, then, reinforce the idea of social life as pretense, artificiality, and role-playing.

The conventional social scene that serves as background to both "Portrait of a Lady" and "Prufrock" illustrates the stereotyped nature of human intercourse and the difficulty of breaking down the barriers between people. Hugh Kenner suggests that Eliot's preoccupation with social behavior

> is related to his early perception that social ritual, designed to permit human beings to associate without imposing on one another . . . may be actually the occasion of raising to nearly tragic intensity their longing to reach one another. The Eliot character feels that he needs to preserve the inviolacy of self and simultaneously feels that he needs sympathy from others whom he cannot reach and who cannot decorously reach him.[16]

When the young man returns in October with a "sensation of being ill at ease"—not that he had seemed at ease on his previous visits—he specifically mentions that he mounts "the stairs"—always a symbol of emotional strife in Eliot's poems (Kenner, 28). His uncomfortable smile "falls heavily among the bric-à-brac," as the lady pretends to accept with equanimity his decision to go abroad (partly perhaps to escape from her), as something from which he will benefit ("'You will find so much to learn'"). Then she returns to her usual theme: "'I have been wondering frequently of late / . . . Why we have not developed into friends'"— another patently misleading remark, since they *are* (merely) friends. At this point his unease becomes so extreme that he feels "like one who smiles, and turning shall remark / Suddenly, his expression in a glass"—a quote that points up the distinction between the inner self and the outer, social self seen by others, or in a glass. The phrase "My self-possession gutters" refers back to the candles at the beginning of the poem.

The final lines reveal once again the protagonist's lack of assurance (like the last line of Part II: "Are these ideas right or wrong?") and the ambiguous nature of his feelings toward the lady. If she died, he would feel guilty for having left, and so she, perhaps, would "have the advantage, after all"—a kind of posthumous moral advantage. The theme of music returns in the last lines, and is linked with the theme of death by the quotation from the beginning of *Twelfth Night*, "it had a dying fall." The question in the final line, again revealing his insecurity, recalls the lady's claim that youth is cruel and smiles because of a lack of comprehension, as well as the young man's smile falling heavily "among the bric-à-brac" and his sense of alienation like that of someone who sees his smile in a glass. These references to smiles probably also originate in Arnold's poem: "Yes, yes, we know that we can jest, / We know, we know that we can smile!"

"Portrait of a Lady" is an unusual dramatic monologue in that the "I" of the poem represents, not the Lady of the title, but the young man who visits her. He is not identified by name, title, or profession, only as the lady's friend—just as Porphyria's lover, in Browning's poem of that title, is identified by his status as lover of Porphyria. The first-person speaker of "Portrait of a Lady" is not the vague "I" of a lyric poem, whom the reader can easily identify with, or equate with the poet (though the protagonist resembles the young Eliot in some ways), because the young man is placed in a specific dramatic situation and a definite context. His relationship with the lady suffices to define him, and involves him in a dramatic conflict: younger than she is, and relatively free to come and go as he pleases, he nevertheless clearly feels obliged to visit her, or perhaps is drawn to her. Yet he does not enjoy the visits; she embarrasses him by her continual insinuations. When he leaves her room he feels he is making an escape, culminating in his final bid for freedom abroad.

As always in the dramatic monologue, there is an element of narrative, though much slighter than in Browning's poems: the reader feels that there is a story behind the poem, though the poem merely hints at it rather than actually telling it. In a lyric poem like Keats' "Ode to Autumn" (or Eliot's own *Four Quartets*), in contrast, there is no sense of narrative.

The setting of the poem helps to identify the young man: he is a member of a class of society that goes to concerts and discusses Chopin's "soul," that drinks tea in the afternoons, talks about friendship, and travels abroad. He also belongs—or poses at belonging—in a male world of newspapers, bars, tobacco, and current events.

"Portrait of a Lady" is also unusual in that it consists partly of dialogue—the lady's words as reported by the young man—and partly of his inner thoughts, whereas the majority of dramatic monologues—especially Browning's—represent the speech of a protagonist addressed to a silent interlocutor. When the second person occurs in this poem, it is not because a speaker is addressing an auditor, as the Bishop addresses his "nephews." The "You" of line 2 is ambiguous, as we have seen; otherwise, the second person pronoun occurs in passages reporting the lady's speech to the young man ("'How keen you are!'"), or it means "one," or perhaps "you the reader," in "You will see me any morning in the park." The poem's speaker—if we may use that term to refer to the young man—uses the first person, of course, but the poem represents his thoughts and recollections rather than his speech. In other words, "Portrait of a Lady" is a soliloquy, an internal monologue. This is true of other dramatic monologues, Browning's "Soliloquy of the Spanish Cloister," Pound's "Marvoil," at least in its second half, and "The Love Song of J. Alfred Prufrock" if we assume that Prufrock addresses himself in line 1. This does not mean, however, that "Portrait of a Lady" is an interior monologue in the sense used to refer to James Joyce's interior monologues based on the "stream of consciousness." John T. Mayer talks of Eliot's "separation from the dramatic monologue" because, he claims, "The fact that Browning's classic form represents *spoken* speech . . . makes it organized and communicated thought, and not the flow of consciousness we find in Eliot."[17] I would argue that in "Portrait of a Lady" the thought is "organized" no less than in "The Bishop Orders His Tomb": the poem seeks to create an effect, to give the flavor of the young man's relationship with the older woman, and all the lines of the poem, all his thoughts and quotations of the lady's speech, contribute toward that end.

The stream of consciousness technique, in contrast, includes apparently random thoughts without logical connections, that is, whatever happens to cross the speaker's (or thinker's) mind, whether or not it is associated with a particular problem or situation. Even here, of course, the author controls the material, but the impression given is one of total spontaneity. The contrast between such random, arbitrary material and the deliberate choices of a dramatic monologue (even an "interior" one) can be illustrated with reference to descriptions. In a Joycean interior monologue, the character's surroundings often are mentioned in an apparently haphazard way, as they chance to impinge on his consciousness. In "Portrait of a Lady" or "Prufrock," the descriptions are not accidental but linked to the speaker's moods or the effect he seeks to create. The "atmosphere of Juliet's tomb" conveys the candlelit scene but also deliberately foreshadows the end of the poem by evoking the theme of a love-story ending in death, and simultaneously subverts the Lady's pretensions to play the role of Juliet. The lilacs, too, are not a casual detail noted by the mind in passing but are highly symbolic, signifying spring, of course, and also—most aptly in connection with this lady—sentimentality and love. In fact, the significant descriptive details that Eliot chooses in this poem constitute examples of what he calls the "objective correlative": to express a particular mood or emotion, he says, the author must find "a set of objects, a situation, a chain of events which shall be the formula of that *particular* emotion; such that when the external facts, which must terminate in sensory experience, are given, the emotion is immediately evoked."[18] Far from being random or accidental, the objects mentioned—the "four wax candles in the darkened room," the lilacs, the various musical instruments, such as the violins with their "attenuated tones," the "cracked cornets," the "broken violin," and the street piano—all evoke a particular idea or mood. The reader does not get the impression that they are there by chance, as in a Joycean monologue based on the stream of consciousness.

Certainly, Eliot's "Prufrock" and "Portrait of a Lady" convey thought rather than speech, and the verse displays some of the free associations typical of thought, for example, when the speaker's mind runs from the content of the newspapers to the street piano and the smell of hyacinths. Yet these items are still part of the whole effect: they suggest that the young man is knowingly acting out a role, and that his apparent self-possession can be punctured by certain sounds and smells, of whose significance he is only vaguely aware. In an attempt to convey the movement of thought, Eliot uses a loose, paratactic syntax; but then so does Browning, to give the impression of oral speech.

The stream of consciousness technique, unlike a dramatic monologue, purports to give all the protagonist's thoughts over a given time span, even those that are totally random and unconnected. Wayne Booth makes this point concerning Stephen's interior monologue in Joyce's *Portrait of the Artist as a Young Man*, which "unlike speech in a dramatic scene" does not "lead us to suspect that the thoughts have been aimed in any way at an effect."[19] Because the discourse of "Portrait of a Lady" is aimed at an effect, like "speech in a dramatic scene," there seems no reason why it should not be called a dramatic monologue. Poetry in general, and certainly "Portrait of a Lady," achieves deliberate effects (by rhyme and rhythm, repetition, use of alliteration, imagery, and symbolism) that are totally alien to the random nature of the stream of consciousness technique;

indeed, it is difficult to see how poetry, which always involves organizational principles of one kind or another, could ever seriously attempt to imitate the disorderly ramblings of the interior monologue. Moreover, the Joycean monologue aims to give the impression of complete spontaneity, whereas the tone of "Portrait of a Lady" is one of all-pervading irony; and irony, far from being spontaneous, suggests a fully conscious, deliberate type of writing.

The refraction of the lady's words through the mind of the young man gives them an ironic slant. This slant comes out in the comparisons he makes—the reference to Juliet's tomb, for example, or his comparison of her voice to an out-of-tune violin—but it is also, more subtly, evident in his reproduction of her speech, with its insistent repetitions and frequent exclamations and rhetorical questions:

> 'You do not know how much they mean to me, my friends,
> And how, how rare and strange it is, to find
> In a life composed so much, so much of odds and ends,
> (For indeed I do not love it . . . you knew? you are not blind!
> How keen you are!)'
> . . . . . . . . . . . . . . . . . .
> 'But what have I, but what have I, my friend,
> To give you, what can you receive from me?'

Practically all her utterances are marked by repetitions of words or phrases: "'Ah, my friend, you do not know, you do not know / What life is"; "You let it flow from you, you let it flow." The young man also mocks her for speaking in clichés, in spite of her air of gushing sincerity—clichés about the qualities of friendship or about spring; the observation that "youth is cruel" and that the young man will "find so much to learn" abroad. He derides her self-pity, too, which comes out in her would-be stoical refrain "'I shall sit here, serving tea to friends.'"

If he is ironic at her expense, he doesn't spare himself, either. Like Prufrock, he is aware of his own lack of assurance, in spite of his "self-possessed" pose. He constantly catches himself playing a role, "like one who smiles, and turning shall remark / Suddenly, his expression in a glass." In the essay "'Rhetoric' and Poetic Drama," Eliot observes that the "really fine rhetoric of Shakespeare occurs in situations where a character in the play *sees himself* in a dramatic light" (*Essays*, 27). Prufrock and the protagonist of "Portrait of a Lady" see themselves this way; they imagine themselves being watched by others.

The reader of Browning's dramatic monologues views his protagonists in an ironic light, but the protagonists take themselves seriously. In other words, the double voice characteristic of the dramatic monologue occurs in the split between the speaker's view of himself and the reader's assessment of him, which of course is engineered by the poet's ingenious arrangement of vocabulary, pauses, hesitations, exclamations, and so on. This "dialogical" discourse, to use Bakhtin's term, "serves two speakers at the same time and expresses simultaneously two different intentions: the direct intention of the character who is speaking, and the refracted intention of the author."[20]

In "Portrait of a Lady" the situation is still more complex: the Lady's words express her direct intention, but, being reported by the young man, are viewed ironically. At the same time, we see the young man in an ironic light, but so does he. Like Prufrock, he is aware of his own shortcomings; both speakers forestall the reader's reaction by judging themselves ironically. Irony and self-parody are signaled in these early poems of Eliot by various devices: repetition, use of clichés, unexpected juxtapositions of words, exaggeration, punctuation (especially ellipsis points), exclamations, and unusual or incongruous rhymes. We have seen that the lady's speech is characterized by her use of repetitions, exclamations, and banal expressions that make the young man squirm with embarrassment. She also affects pretentious words like "bloom," and "*cauchemar*." Her shameless persistence is mocked by the insistent rhyme and by the abruptness of the short sentences in: "We must leave it now to fate. / You will write, at any rate. / Perhaps it is not too late." The young man's own language betrays self-parody:

> Let us take the air, in a tobacco trance,
> Admire the monuments,
> Discuss the late events,
> Correct our watches by the public clocks.
> Then sit for half an hour and drink our bocks.

An ironic intention is signaled here by the incongruous juxtaposition of the notions of taking the air and being in a fog of tobacco smoke; by the insistent chime of the rhymes, "monuments/events" and "clocks/bocks," and by the fatuous self-importance implied in the image of the men wanting to "Correct our watches by the public clocks." Again the speaker mocks himself when he declares "I keep my countenance / I remain self-possessed": his making this statement tends to imply that it is not true. Prufrock, too, is ironic at his own expense, which can emerge simply in his choice of adjectives to describe a tie: "My necktie rich and modest, but asserted by a simple pin"—or in a rhyme: "Should I, after tea and cakes and ices, / Have the strength to force the moment to its crisis?"—or in an image: "I have measured out my life with coffee spoons" and "I shall wear the bottoms of my trousers rolled." He juxtaposes "the cups, the marmalade, the tea" with abstractions concerning the universe and his "overwhelming question"; and the long passage based on the phrase from Ecclesiastes, "There will be time," is followed incongruously by "the taking of a toast and tea." Exclamations, rhetorical questions, and repetitions also imply an ironic stance.

Eliot no doubt owed the discovery of the possibilities of this type of ironic verse to the 19-century French poet Jules Laforgue (1860–1887). Eliot repeatedly stated his admiration for Laforgue and his feeling that the discovery of the French poet opened up new avenues for him.[21] In poems that approximate closely to dramatic monologues—though the genre as such was unknown in France—Laforgue adopts various masks and disguises to express his feelings of loneliness, yearning, irritation, despair, boredom, or indifference. The question of identity looms large in his poetry; the self is seen as fragmented and multiple, as in this example from "Ballade" (in *Des Fleurs de bonne volonté*):

> Quand j'organise une descente en Moi,
> J'en conviens, je trouve là, attablée,
> Une société un peu bien mêlée . . . .
>
> (When I decide to drop in on Myself,
> I must admit I find there, round the table,
> Quite a mixed company of people.)

One of Laforgue's most common personae is Pierrot, or, incongruously, "Lord Pierrot," a figure who combines seriousness with playfulness, as in the "Complainte de Lord Pierrot" from *Les Complaintes*:

Ma cervelle est morte.
Que le Christ l'emporte!
Béons à la Lune
La bouche en zéro.
Inconscient, descendez en nous par réflexes;
Brouillez les cartes, les dictionnaires, les sexes . . . .
J'ai le coeur chase et vrai comme une bonne lampe.

(My brain is dead
Christ take it! So
Let's gaze at the moon
With our mouths in an O. [These lines parody the
     famous song "Au clair de la lune"]
Come down to us, Unconscious, through our reflexes;
Mix up the cards, the dictionaries and sexes . . . .
My heart is chaste and true like a trusty lamp.)

Pierrot cannot sustain the same self-image for long; expressions of apparently genuine emotion, such as the last line above, are at once deflated by a mocking voice.

In order to achieve his ironic effects, Laforgue uses devices such as repetition, punctuation (ellipsis points, italics, quotation marks), deliberate clichés, exclamations, unexpected rhymes, and incongruous juxtapositions of words—all of which abound in his poems. Many of these devices were adopted later by Eliot, though he is more restrained in his use of such features. Laforgue's women speakers, like the lady in "Portrait of a Lady," constantly harp on the theme of love, trying to "catch" a man, while the men are more reticent. In "Autre complainte de Lord Pierrot" ("Another Complaint of Lord Pierrot"), Pierrot openly mocks the lady's claims; when she declares "'Tu te lasseras le premier, j'en suis sûre . . .'" ("'You will get tired of me first, I'm sure'"), he responds with a cliché from another context that makes sense here too: "'Après vous, s'il vous plaît'" ("'After you, please'"—or, as one might translate it, "'Ladies first, please'"). In "Pierrots," from L'Imitation de Notre-Dame la lune, he hypocritically adopts the rhetoric traditionally associated with love to declare: "Ange! tu m'as compris, / A la vie, à la mort!" ("Angel! you understand me, / Till death do us part!")—while secretly thinking: "Ah! passer là-dessus l'éponge! . . ." ("Oh! Let's have done with this! . . ."). Laforgue's male speakers, like Prufrock or the protagonist of "Portrait of a Lady," act out a part, while mocking themselves for doing so, as Pierrot's incongruous comparison of himself with a dog reveals in the following lines from "Locutions des Pierrots, I":

> Voilà tantôt une heure qu'en langueur
> Mon coeur si simple s'abreuve
> De vos vilaines rigueurs,
> Avec le regard bon d'un terre-neuve.

> (For an hour now my heart so simple and
> So good, has languished here,
> Lapping up your wicked cruelties
> With the trusting gaze of a newfoundland.)

If the male protagonists of Laforgue's poems act out different roles, it is partly because they have no sense of their own personality: "j'allais me donner d'un 'Je vous aime,'" declares the speaker of *Derniers vers* III, "Quand je m'avisai non sans peine / Que d'abord je ne me possédais pas bien moi-même." ("I was about to come out with an 'I love you' / When I realized, with something of a pang, / That I couldn't even say I owned myself.") Eliot went further than Laforgue in questioning the whole notion of character as a fixed, knowable quantity—partly, perhaps, thanks to his study of the philosopher F.C. Bradley, who rejected the notion of personality, insisting that "the usual self of one period is not the usual self of another" (quoted in Kenner, 59), and that each individual is, in any case, unknowable, "opaque" to others, as he says in the paragraph quoted by Eliot in the Notes to *The Waste Land*. Eliot's speakers impress the reader not as characters with a distinct personality of their own, like most of Browning's protagonists, but as a "zone of consciousness," a consciousness that sees, hears, records, and reflects, but does not reveal the developed personality of, say, the Bishop. In some ways, Eliot's monologues resemble Tennyson's far more than Browning's: "Like Tennyson," as Carol Christ says, "Eliot is less interested in creating particular historical characters than in using character to delimit a zone of consciousness" (Christ, 47). Pound followed Browning in choosing to bring to life historical characters as the subjects of his dramatic monologues (though as we have seen he was more interested in reproducing the intensity of such a character's "moment of song" than in a complete study), but Eliot's speakers, like Tennyson's, belong to the universal realm of myth rather than to history. In *The Waste Land* he uses the Grail legend as background; and the speakers in that poem, like Prufrock or the protagonist of "Portrait of a Lady," have a mythical, archetypical dimension, despite their modernity. As George T. Wright suggests, most of Eliot's personae "are drawn from modern European culture, and much of the point in their actions lies in the juxtapositions within them of contemporary and eternal human qualities."[22] A comparison with Pound's *Cantos* is instructive: Eliot, with the ladies in the pub, the typist, Mr. Eugenides, and Prufrock, creates quasi-mythical figures, "*types* of modern decadence," whose "historical existence is irrelevant"; whereas Pound deals with historical figures giving voice to a multitude of *individuals:* politicians, scientists, artists, painters, and so on; his method is narrative rather than mythical.[23]

Eliot, as he himself says of Tennyson (*Essays*, 289), uses narrative merely to create a mood, or as a vehicle for exploring a consciousness from the *inside.* Carol Christ remarks that, like Tennyson, "Eliot is . . . very much preoccupied with the pains and indulgences of the solitary ego"—a typically 20th-century ego. She concludes that the "characteristic voice of Eliot's early monologues results in part from his combination" of two registers present in Tennyson: the social satire that underlies poems like *Maud* and "Locksley Hall," and "the mythological resonance of 'Tithonus' or 'Ulysses'" (Christ, 48). Critics might claim that Eliot found his social satire in Laforgue rather than in Tennyson, but Eliot's mature poetry, if it resembles anyone's, sounds more like Tennyson than either Browning or Laforgue.

Although Eliot's syntax is never as literary as Tennyson's, there are moments when he moves from his basically oral idiom to a more "written" style, for example, in lines like "I feel like one who smiles, and turning shall remark / Suddenly, his expression in a glass," which then conclude with the colloquial phrase "we are really in the dark." This movement is found in later poetry too, such as the following passage from "Burnt Norton" in *Four Quartets,* where the measured, literary flow of the first four lines is interrupted by the more excitable, less coherent syntax of the next section:

> . . . Only by the form, the pattern,
> Can words or music reach

> The stillness, as a Chinese jar still
> Moves perpetually in its stillness.
> Not the stillness of the violin, while the note lasts,
> Not that only, but the co-existence,
> Or say that the end precedes the beginning
> And the end and the beginning were always there
> Before the beginning and after the end.

Again, if Eliot basically keeps to the rhythms and intonations of speech, he nevertheless retains for the most part, like Tennyson, a certain dignity of tone: unlike Pound or Browning—or Laforgue—he avoids outright colloquialisms, slang expressions, too-frequent exclamations, or interjections such as "Ah, God!" or "Bah!" Also, like Tennyson, he pays far more attention than Browning to the musical qualities of poetry, as in the passage from "Burnt Norton" partially quoted above, and which begins

> Words move, music moves
> Only in time; but that which is only living
> Can only die. Words, after speech, reach
> Into the silence.

The musical repetitions, alliterations, and rhythms of this passage, with its many run-on lines, reinforce the sense of the words—the idea of reaching after perfection, and the beauty of stillness and silence. The "mermaids" section of "Prufrock" also contains lines whose music (sounds and rhythm) reinforces the image:

> I have seen them riding seaward on the waves
> Combing the white hair of the waves blown back
> When the wind blows the water white and black.

"Portrait of a Lady" contains some musical lines, such as "Afternoon grey and smoky, evening yellow and rose," with its carefully-modulated rhythm, or the first two lines of Part II with their alliteration of *b* and *l* sounds and the repeated "-oom" rhyme: "Now that lilacs are in bloom / She has a bowl of lilacs in her room." This rhyme is echoed repeatedly in the first dozen lines of the poem, appearing once, sinisterly, as "tomb"; and it contrasts with the sharp *k* and *t* sounds of the following lines: "Among velleities and carefully-caught regrets / Through attenuated tones of violins / Mingled with remote cornets." It is typical of Eliot to use a learned word like "velleities" (vague wishes or inclinations) in lines whose rhythm is essentially that of oral speech.

The rhyme-scheme of the poem is irregular; most lines rhyme, sometimes in an *abba* pattern, sometimes *abab*, sometimes in couplets, and occasionally at a distance (for example, "finger-tips" and "slips"). The word "friends," so often repeated by the lady, frequently rhymes, pessimistically, with "ends." Rhyme can give an impression of conclusiveness and decision in a world otherwise composed so much of hesitation, doubts, and half-expressed thoughts, for example, when the young man declares, "My self-possession flares up for a second; / *This* is as I had reckoned," or when he evokes the male world of clocks and bocks.

"Portrait of a Lady," as most of Eliot's poetry, is written in free verse, with the length of each line determined by the length of the thought or phrase rather than by a fixed meter. Like the poem's speaker, it "borrows every changing shape / To find expression." Nevertheless, as Eliot himself points out, "no verse is free for the man who wants to do a good job," and "only a bad poet could welcome free verse as a liberation from form." It was "a revolt against dead form," but it still provides a rhythmic structure.[24] Free verse allows Eliot to achieve a variety of rhythmic effects, and in particular to take advantage of contrasts between long and short lines. The lady's lines tend to be long, reflecting her prolixity, whereas the man responds, "I smile, of course, / And go on drinking tea." The lines relating what he reads in the newspapers are also short and matter-of-fact, until he hears the street-piano and waxes lyrical, and the lines lengthen. Use of free verse enhances the impression of a conversational style—both in Eliot and in Laforgue, one of the first poets in France to employ free verse. This impression is reinforced by the punctuation, such as the exclamations and question marks (". . . you knew? you are not blind!"), the dashes signifying changes of topic or syntactic elisions, the spaced points indicating hesitations or insinuations ("I shall sit here serving tea to friends . . . .").

"Portrait of a Lady," like "The Love Song of J. Alfred Prufrock," is an early poem, written when Eliot was under the spell of Laforgue. In his later work, Eliot abandoned Laforgue's permanently ironic stance (as the French poet might also have done, had he lived long enough) in favor of a more serious and meditative style. He also gradually abandoned the use of dramatic monologue. *The Waste Land* still enacts personae, but they are multiple and fragmented. In *Four Quartets* there is no longer any trace of persona or of personality. We simply hear a voice, located in no particular time or space (except insofar as the poems' titles suggest places), meditating on a wide range of subjects: time, memory, human behavior, language, love, life. The poem presents the contents of a mind, but the mind is not attributed to anyone in particular.

A change in poetic diction accompanies this progressive depersonalization of the speaker in Eliot. Gone is the Laforguian tone of the early poems, the irony, the use of clichés, the punctuation—exclamations, quotation marks, dashes, and ellipsis points—that Eliot had in any case always used more sparingly than Laforgue. What remains is the intonation of a voice speaking on serious topics, and the impression of the speaking voice is created not by the use of punctuation and exclamations but simply by rhythm and syntax. As noted above, in the Overview of the dramatic monologue, the voice of *Four Quartets*, even when treating the most abstract or literary topics, often in a learned vocabulary, generally retains the rhythms and syntactical constructions of oral speech, as in the following lines from "Burnt Norton":

> ....................... And do not call it fixity,
> Where past and future are gathered. Neither movement from nor
>     towards,
> Neither ascent nor decline. Except for the point, the still point,
> There would be no dance, and there is only the dance.
> I can only say, *there* we have been: but I cannot say where.

While retaining the cadences of speech, the verse of *Four Quartets* is also remarkable for its musical qualities. Eliot criticized the French poet Paul Valéry for valuing musicality in poetry at the expense of spoken language: "In assimilating poetry to music, Valéry has, it seems to me, failed to insist upon its relation to speech."[25] Eliot insists on the importance of both, in his essay on "The Music of Poetry," even remarking how it may seem strange "that when I profess to be talking about the 'music' of poetry, I put such emphasis upon conversation." He states here, as a categorical law, that "poetry must not stray too far from the ordinary everyday language which we use and hear" (*On Poetry and Poets,* 21). Certainly his own late poetry evokes the rhythms of speech—of serious, intelligent speech—without sacrificing the musical qualities of the verse.

*Four Quartets* is the work of a mature poet who has found a voice that, without revealing himself personally, is his alone—and yet dwells on universal aspects of human experience. The voice of the poem moves, as Kenner puts it, "from exposition through intimacy to reminiscence, passing through lyric, expending itself in overheard meditation, without ever allowing us to intuit the impurities of personal presence" (294). Eliot insisted that "the emotion of art is impersonal" (*Essays,* 11)—though his use of the terms "personal" and "impersonal" is imprecise and sometimes contradictory.[26] Clearly, however, in his early dramatic monologues, the use of a persona had helped to achieve that "escape from personality" (*Essays,* 10) that he saw as essential for the poet; and by the time of *Four Quartets* the mature Eliot had found a voice to "transmute his personal and private agonies into something . . . universal and impersonal" (*Essays,* 117).

Chapter 4

# OTHER TWENTIETH-CENTURY PRACTITIONERS OF THE DRAMATIC MONOLOGUE

## A Brief Survey

Although the heyday of the dramatic monologue was the late 19th century, there are many examples in the 20th century, especially in American poetry. We will examine in detail two poems, by Robert Frost and Richard Howard; but first let us look briefly at a few dramatic monologues by other 20th-century poets, both British and American.

D.H. Lawrence wrote many dramatic monologues, including the short but poignant "A Youth Mowing," a soliloquy presenting the thoughts of a girl concerning the youth who has made her pregnant but does not yet know it. W.H. Auden's "Refugee Blues" from *Another Time* (1940) is spoken by a German Jew: "Once we had a country and we thought it fair, / Look in the atlas and you'll find it there: / We cannot go there now, my dear, we cannot go there now."

An unusual dramatic monologue by a British poet is Ted Hughes' short but splendid poem "Hawk Roosting," from *Lupercal* (1960), in which the speaker is a hawk. He sits "in the top of the wood," from where he can survey the entire world and swoop down on his prey. He rejoices in his power and perfection: "It took the whole of Creation / To produce my foot, my each feather: / Now I hold Creation in my foot." The poem emphasizes the hawk's predatory instincts and desire to dominate, which are presented as fact rather than in moral terms. His supremacy is not open to discussion; that is simply the way things are, and he is determined to "keep things like this."

Another, very different, dramatic monologue by a British poet is Philip Larkin's "Wedding-Wind" from *XX Poems* (1951). Like many 20th-century monologues, the poem gives the protagonist's thoughts, rather than her speech: in other words, no interlocutor is present. A bride describes how the wind blew on her wedding day and into the night; her husband had to get up to shut a banging door "leaving me / Stupid in candlelight, hearing rain, / Seeing my face in the twisted candlestick, / Yet seeing nothing." This sense of unease pervades the rest of the poem, attenuating the bride's feelings of joy and sexual fulfillment.

Turning now to American poetry, the work of Edwin Arlington Robinson (1869–1935) displays a keen interest in human psychology, revealed in his many dramatic poems and dialogues. Several of the longer poems are dramatic monologues, in blank verse, including "The Three Taverns," "John Brown," and "Ben Jonson Entertains a Man from Stratford." In "Rembrandt to Rembrandt (Amsterdam, 1645)," the painter addresses himself, looking in a mirror, so that speaker and interlocutor are identical—an arrangement that forms an interesting parallel with Rembrandt's self-portraits. This soliloquy takes place at a low point in Rembrandt's career, when his art is no longer admired by society, which leads him to describe himself as "Sometime a personage in Amsterdam, / But now not much." However, he retains his confidence in his artistic integrity and skill: ". . . Well, if God knows, / And Rembrandt knows, it matters not so much / What Holland knows or cares." As in some of Browning's poems, the spatial and temporal context is indicated in the title ("Amsterdam, 1645"), as well as by details in the body of the poem.

"Rembrandt to Rembrandt" appears in *Avon's Harvest* (1921). A later collection, *Nicodemus* (1932), contains another long dramatic monologue, "Toussaint l'Ouverture (Chateau de Joux, 1803)," in which Toussaint, shortly before his death, mourns the fate of Haiti ("My lost friends! My island!"). He describes his struggle with Napoleon over freedom for Haitian blacks: "France was a place where they were starving me / To death, because a black man had a brain"; "Last night I saw Napoleon in hell. / . . . / . . . I could see that hate / For me was still alive in his blind eyes." Joux is the name of the fortress where Toussaint was imprisoned and where he died in 1803.

These are powerful works that evoke the personalities and situations of recognizable historical figures; very different are the dramatic monologues of Edgar Lee Masters (1868–1950) in his *Spoon River Anthology* (1915). Masters wrote many other volumes of poetry both before and after this one, but this was his only really successful collection. It consists of 214 epitaphs spoken from beyond the grave by deceased men and women from the imaginary small town of Spoon River. Thus they are all monologues; most of them are short, and the lines are also quite short, of no fixed length, and unrhymed. The rhythms, syntax, and vocabulary are those of oral speech, and the language of each poem is characteristic of its speaker. Many of the poems evoke mundane incidents from small-town life; but each poem also centers on a dramatic event in the speaker's life. Knowlt Hoheimer was killed in the battle of Missionary Ridge and claims that "When I felt the bullet enter my heart / I wished I had staid at home and gone to jail / For stealing the hogs of Curl Trenary." He would have much preferred the county jail to "this granite pedestal / Bearing the words, '*Pro Patria.*' / What do they mean, anyway?" The effects of industrialization on a small town are suggested in several poems, including "'Butch' Weldy," who describes an accident that took place at the canning factory where he started working, he says, "After I got religion and steadied down." One day he was injured when a gasoline tank exploded: both legs broken "And my eyes burned crisp as a couple of eggs"; he received no compensation.

Amy Lowell's works include many dramatic monologues, such as "Patterns" from the volume with the somewhat

Browningesque title of *Men, Women and Ghosts* (1916). "Appuldurcombe Park" from *Pictures of the Floating World* (1919) presents a similar persona: a lonely woman, "sick for passion"; "And all day long my husband calls me / From his invalid chair / "Mary, Mary, where are you, Mary? I want you."

Louis Untermeyer's *Selected Poems and Parodies* (1935) contains several dramatic monologues, such as "Eve Speaks" and "Moses on Sinai" from *These Times* (1917), and the "Monolog from a Mattress" from *Roast Leviathan* (1923), in which "Heinrich Heine, 56, speaks." The style of this poem displays the wit and sense of irony that are typical of Heine's own poetry.

Langston Hughes has written dramatic monologues drawing attention to the problems of black people, such as "The Negro Speaks of Rivers" (1921), and "Merry-Go-Round," in which the little colored child asks "Where's the horse for the kid that's black?"

Allen Tate's *Collected Poems 1919–1976* includes several dramatic monologues, such as "Aeneas at Washington" (1933) and "Aeneas at New York"; "To the Lacedemonians" (1932), in which an old soldier "talks partly to himself, partly to imaginary comrades"; and "Lycambes Talks to John (in Hell)" (1923), where the Greek Lycambes offers an Oedipal explanation as to why he refused to let his daughter marry Archilochus.

Robert Lowell's early collections, *Lord Weary's Castle* (1946) and *The Mills of the Kavanaughs* (1951), contain several dramatic monologues. Two of them, "Mr. Edwards and the Spider" and "After the Surprising Conversions," are spoken by the 18th-century Calvinist Jonathan Edwards, whose sermons dwelt on sin and punishment and God's wrath. In "Mr. Edwards and the Spider," Edwards addresses his cousin, Josiah Hawley, who committed suicide after listening to his sermons. The spiders he describes symbolize man's helplessness "in the hands of the great God"; his obsession with damnation and hellfire comes out strongly in the poem, as well as a morbid preoccupation with death and human awareness of death: "the blaze / Is infinite, eternal: this is death, / To die and know it. This is the Black Widow, death." The final metaphor returns us to the image of spiders at the beginning of the poem.

Another, very successful, dramatic monologue by Lowell is "Mother Marie Therese" from *The Mills of the Kavanaughs*. As in Eliot's "Portrait of a Lady," the speaker is not the person suggested by the title, but "a Canadian nun stationed in New Brunswick," and the poem consists of her reflections on the life of the (fictional) Mother Marie Therese, who drowned in 1912. This point of view allows the reader to perceive aspects of the nun's character, as well as that of Mother Marie Therese, and to imagine the interaction of the two. Mother Marie Therese came from an aristocratic European family, was accustomed to hunting and reading Rabelais, and was interested in the politics of the French succession. She represents a bygone era and a style of living totally foreign to convents and to the nun who speaks, whose admiration for Mother Marie Therese is tempered with puzzlement. The nun does not explain how Marie Therese came to drown "on an excursion," but she dwells on the thought of her dead body afloat now in the ocean, where "The bell-buoy, whom she called the Cardinal, / Dances upon her." The sexual overtones of this passage are reinforced by the suggestion, a few lines later, that the nuns' "stern virginity" is "*Contra naturam.*" This poem is composed in rhyming couplets, though at the end there are eight lines all sharing basically the same rhyme, as if to embody the echoes evoked there of times gone by.

Randall Jarrell's works include several dramatic monologues spoken by children or women. Among the war poems in his *Selected Poems* (1955), "The State" and "The Truth" show the reactions of two children to the way the war has affected their lives. According to a note by Jarrell, the boy in "The Truth" speaks from a mental institution for children, in the country, where he has been sent to escape the air raids over London. He was four years old when his father "went to Scotland," as they told him, though actually he had been killed in the war; also, his dog and his sister died in air raids, but he was never told and has become very disturbed because of his mother's deception. Finally, before his confused accusations, his mother breaks down and sobs "Yes, he's dead, he's dead!" and at last the boy is able to recognize that she at least is left to him, and to release his pent-up emotions in tears: "she *was* my mother, / She put her arms around me and we cried."

Jarrell's later collections contain several powerful, poignant dramatic monologues with women speakers. "The Lost Children," from *The Lost World* (1965) is based on a dream of the poet's wife Mary, as well as on a story by Rudyard Kipling entitled "They." In the poem, a woman dreams about her two little daughters, and then, on waking, reflects on what has become of them—both the dark one, who died, and the fair one, who is still alive but married and with a life of her own. The mother looks back fondly at the time in her memory before she "lost" them both, a time when they made demands and "begged to follow you / Anywhere, just so long as it was you." Any parent can identify with the sense of loss involved in this scenario.

"Next Day," also from *The Lost World*, has a somewhat similar theme, except that here the speaker places more emphasis on the pain of aging and the apprehension of death. This poem opens in a supermarket, where the speaker, "Moving from Cheer to Joy, from Joy to All," takes a box and adds it to her purchases. The cheerful names of the products contrast with her mood as she realizes that no one looks at her any more: once beautiful and desirable, she is now old. In her youth she always wished for a husband and family, and she has had them; but now the children are away at school, and she misses them. The title of the poem, "Next Day," refers to the fact that the previous day she attended the funeral of a friend, which has reminded her of her own mortality: "I stand beside my grave / Confused with my life, that is commonplace and solitary."

A somewhat earlier work, "The Woman at the Washington Zoo," from the collection of the same title (1960), is a magnificent poem that also bemoans a "commonplace and solitary" life. The woman here is identified, not by name, but as an office worker in Washington, walking through the zoo probably on her way home. Washington is evoked by the mention of domes, columns, and fountains. She characterizes herself and her life by the color of her clothes—accentuated by alliteration: "this dull null / Navy I wear to work, and wear from work"; her navy blue outfit contrasts strongly with the bright colors of the saris that go by her "from the embassies." She refers to her body in similar terms as to her clothes: "this serviceable / Body that no sunlight dyes, no hand suffuses . . . ." Her longing for sexual fulfillment bursts out in the cry "Oh, bars of my own body, open, open!" where, again, the sense is reinforced by assonance and alliteration. The woman compares herself to the caged animals, with the difference that "The world goes by my cage and never sees me." The animals, moreover, are unaware of being trapped in the process of aging, unaware of the death that awaits them; consciousness, the supreme attribute of mankind, is also a source of anguish. The woman is afraid she will die without ever experiencing Life. She longs for a visitation from a man—a man "To whose hand of power the great lioness / Stalks, purring." In this part of the poem bright colors appear again: the "red helmet" and "black / Wings" of the vulture that snatches a "white rat" from a cage. This again contrasts with her colorlessness, even invisibility: no one sees her in her "cage."

"The Woman at the Washington Zoo" comprises some thirty lines of pentameters, or approximate pentameters, unrhymed, though there are many repeated words and sounds. Occasional gaps between the lines add emphasis or give pause for reflection. The words "And I . . ." for example, stand alone on the page, as she compares her drabness with the saris' "Cloth from the moon." The desperation of her cry "Oh, bars of my own body, open, open!" is emphasized by the space following.

Jarrell himself produced a commentary on this poem in his volume of essays *A Sad Heart at the Supermarket* (1962). He mentions some biographical background—he had recently moved to Washington with his family, often visited the zoo, and often saw women like the one he describes. He also analyzes the poem's initial conception and development: it grew from the notion of a colorless, drab life and drab clothes ("this dull null / Navy I wear to work"), contrasted later with the colors of other women's clothes and of the zoo. Placing the woman in the zoo enabled him to introduce ideas of imprisonment, and also of violent sexuality, which were relevant to the subject. Jarrell's essay gives an interesting account of a poet's view of the growth of his own poem.

Turning now to the dramatic monologues we will analyze in detail, let us look at poems by two American poets: first, Robert Frost's "A Servant to Servants," and then a poem by a contemporary poet, Richard Howard.

## Robert Frost

"At his death in January 1963 Frost was without question his country's most-read, most-celebrated, most-beloved poet," states Edward Connery Lathem, editor of Frost's poetry.[1] In a long lifetime (1874–1963) that almost parallels that of Eliot, Frost produced several volumes of poetry. A resident of Massachusetts,

Vermont, and New Hampshire for most of his life (though born in San Francisco), Frost found a frequent source of inspiration in the scenery, customs, and people of New England, as the titles of some of his collections witness: *North of Boston, Mountain Interval, New Hampshire, West-Running Brook, A Witness Tree, Steeple Bush,* and *In the Clearing.*

Frost's poetic career got off to a slow start; he had trouble publishing his early poems and in 1912 he moved to England, with his wife and four children, in search of a more congenial and stimulating literary climate. Like Eliot, Frost met Pound in London, who reviewed his early poetry; he also became associated with various British literary figures. He quickly published *A Boy's Will* (1913), and *North of Boston* (1914), first in England and then in America, and he returned to the United States in 1915 with the beginnings of a reputation. He divided his time thereafter between writing poetry, teaching, and, in a modest way, farming.

The poem we will examine in detail, "A Servant to Servants," appears in the early collection *North of Boston* and is the only true dramatic monologue in the volume, though many of the poems, in this collection as in others, have strong narrative and dramatic qualities. "Everything written is as good as it is dramatic," declares Frost, and in this he agrees with Eliot, who asks in "A Dialogue on Dramatic Poetry" "what great poetry is not dramatic?"[2] Many of Frost's poems are not only dramatic in subject matter and treatment but are composed largely in dialogue form, with sections in quotation marks. The celebrated "Home Burial," for example, is basically a dramatic dialogue, within a narrative framework, between a husband and wife who express very different reactions to the loss of a child. The equally famous poem "The Death of the Hired Man" also presents a dialogue between husband and wife and contains a strong narrative element. "Mending Wall," a monologue and another much-anthologized poem, reads almost like a dramatic monologue, except that the speaker is not identified in any other way than as a farmer. A reader unaware that Frost often lived on farms could read the poem as a dramatic monologue, with a farmer as speaker; whereas when one knows that Frost lived most of his life on farms there is a strong tendency to equate the "I" of the poem with the persona of the poet. Frost himself suggested that "Maybe [he] was both fellows in the poem," though one concludes his views were much closer to those of the speaker than to those of the neighbor.[3]

"Mending Wall," like so many of Frost's poems, reveals an interest in other people and the relations among them, and an attitude of affectionate, amused tolerance for them. Very often they are New Englanders, placed in New England scenery, though they certainly illustrate human nature in general and often enact universal human joys and tragedies—like the protagonists of "Home Burial" who grapple with the loss of their dead child, a loss that threatens to undermine their whole relationship and possibly the wife's sanity. Along with this concern for ordinary people goes a liking for realistic, concrete details and for "plain speech." The diction of his poems usually is very natural-sounding and matter-of-fact, as in the lines about the property the wall divides, in "Mending Wall": "He is all pine and I am appple orchard. / My apple trees will never get across / And eat the cones under his pines, I tell him." Concrete details evoked in a spoken idiom nevertheless may be invested with significant or symbolic meaning, like the two roads that "diverged in a yellow wood" in "The Road Not Taken"; but the language itself has the directness of everyday speech. The rhythms, syntax, and phrasing, too, have a conversational quality that makes the reader forget that Frost's poetry is written, for the most part, in iambic pentameters, that is, five feet, each containing one unstressed syllable followed by a stressed one.

English poetry, says Frost, has "virtually but two" meters—"strict iambic and loose iambic" (*Selected Prose*, 17–18). Most of his long poems are written in blank verse—without the benefit of rhyme—but the "loose iambic" rhythm is there, playing against the informal, oral tone of the diction. As Frost himself points out, the "possibilities for tune from the dramatic tones of meaning struck across the rigidity of a limited meter are endless" (*Selected Prose*, 18). In the opening lines of "Mending Wall," ("Something there is that doesn't love a wall, / That sends the frozen ground-well under it / And spills the upper boulders in the sun, / And makes gaps even two can pass abreast"), the second and third lines have a regular iambic beat, whereas the first and fourth lines include beats that are displaced from the iambic norm in order to create variety, enhance the impression of oral diction, and, no doubt, to demonstrate the force that makes gaps through which "two can pass." Despite the iambic pentameters, in this and other poems of Frost's the overall impression is of a person speaking.

"A Servant to Servants," too, is composed in blank verse with a "loose iambic" rhythm. The speaker is the "Servant" of the title—though she is not addressing servants:

A SERVANT TO SERVANTS

I didn't make you know how glad I was
To have you come and camp here on our land.
I promised myself to get down some day
And see the way you lived, but I don't know!
With a houseful of hungry men to feed                    5
I guess you'd find .... It seems to me
I can't express my feelings, any more
Than I can raise my voice or want to lift
My hand (oh, I can lift it when I have to).
Did ever you feel so? I hope you never.                  10
It's got so I don't even know for sure
Whether I *am* glad, sorry, or anything.
There's nothing but a voice-like left inside
That seems to tell me how I ought to feel,
And would feel if I wasn't all gone wrong.               15
You take the lake. I look and look at it.
I see it's a fair, pretty sheet of water.
I stand and make myself repeat out loud
The advantages it has, so long and narrow,
Like a deep piece of some old running river              20
Cut short off at both ends. It lies five miles
Straightaway through the mountain notch
From the sink window where I wash the plates,
And all our storms come up toward the house,
Drawing the slow waves whiter and whiter and whiter.     25
It took my mind off doughnuts and soda biscuit
To step outdoors and take the water dazzle
A sunny morning, or take the rising wind
About my face and body and through my wrapper,
When a storm threatened from the Dragon's Den,           30
And a cold chill shivered across the lake.
I see it's a fair, pretty sheet of water,
Our Willoughby! How did you hear of it?
I expect, though, everyone's heard of it.
In a book about ferns? Listen to that!                   35
You let things more like feathers regulate

Your going and coming. And you like it here?
I can see how you might. But I don't know!
It would be different if more people came,
For then there would be business. As it is,                    40
The cottages Len built, sometimes we rent them,
Sometimes we don't. We've a good piece of shore
That ought to be worth something, and may yet.
But I don't count on it as much as Len.
He looks on the bright side of everything,                     45
Including me. He thinks I'll be all right
With doctoring. But it's not medicine—
Lowe is the only doctor's dared to say so—
It's rest I want—there, I have said it out—
From cooking meals for hungry hired men                        50
And washing dishes after them—from doing
Things over and over that just won't stay done.
By good rights I ought not to have so much
Put on me, but there seems no other way.
Len says one steady pull more ought to do it.                  55
He says the best way out is always through.
And I agree to that, or in so far
As that I can see no way out but through—
Leastways for me—and then they'll be convinced.
It's not that Len don't want the best for me.                  60
It was his plan our moving over in
Beside the lake from where that day I showed you
We used to live—ten miles from anywhere.
We didn't change without some sacrifice,
But Len went at it to make up the loss.                        65
His work's a man's, of course, from sun to sun,
But he works when he works as hard as I do
Though there's small profit in comparisons.
(Women and men will make them all the same.)
But work ain't all. Len undertakes too much.                  70
He's into everything in town. This year
It's highways, and he's got too many men
Around him to look after that make waste.
They take advantage of him shamefully,
And proud, too, of themselves for doing so.                    75
We have four here to board, great good-for-nothings,
Sprawling about the kitchen with their talk
While I fry their bacon. Much they care!
No more put out in what they do or say
Than if I wasn't in the room at all.                           80

Coming and going all the time, they are:
I don't learn what their names are, let alone
Their characters, or whether they are safe
To have inside the house with doors unlocked.
I'm not afraid of them, though, if they're not          85
Afraid of me. There's two can play at that.
I have my fancies: it runs in the family.
My father's brother wasn't right. They kept him
Locked up for years back there at the old farm.
I've been away once—yes, I've been away.           90
The State Asylum. I was prejudiced;
I wouldn't have sent anyone of mine there;
You know the old idea—the only asylum
Was the poorhouse, and those who could afford,
Rather than send their folks to such a place,           95
Kept them at home; and it does seem more human.
But it's not so: the place is the asylum.
There they have every means proper to do with,
And you aren't darkening other people's lives—
Worse than no good to them, and they no good          100
To you in your condition; you can't know
Affection or the want of it in that state.
I've heard too much of the old-fashioned way.
My father's brother, he went mad quite young
Some thought he had been bitten by a dog,           105
Because his violence took on the form
Of carrying his pillow in his teeth;
But it's more likely he was crossed in love,
Or so the story goes. It was some girl.
Anyway all he talked about was love.           110
They soon saw he would do someone a mischief
If he wa'n't kept strict watch of, and it ended
In father's building him a sort of cage,
Or room within a room, of hickory poles,
Like stanchions in the barn, from floor to ceiling—           115
A narrow passage all the way around.
Anything they put in for furniture
He'd tear to pieces, even a bed to lie on.
So they made the place comfortable with straw,
Like a beast's stall, to ease their consciences.           120
Of course they had to feed him without dishes.
They tried to keep him clothed, but he paraded
With his clothes on his arm—all of his clothes.
Cruel—it sounds. I s'pose they did the best

They knew. And just when he was at the height,     125
Father and mother married, and mother came,
A bride, to help take care of such a creature,
And accommodate her young life to his.
That was what marrying father meant to her.
She had to lie and hear love things made dreadful     130
By his shouts in the night. He'd shout and shout
Until the strength was shouted out of him,
And his voice died down slowly from exhaustion.
He'd pull his bars apart like bow and bowstring,
And let them go and make them twang, until     135
His hands had worn them smooth as any oxbow.
And then he'd crow as if he thought that child's play—
The only fun he had. I've heard them say, though,
They found a way to put a stop to it.
He was before my time—I never saw him;     140
But the pen stayed exactly as it was,
There in the upper chamber in the ell,
A sort of catchall full of attic clutter.
I often think of the smooth hickory bars.
It got so I would say—you know, half fooling—     145
"It's time I took my turn upstairs in jail"
Just as you will till it becomes a habit.
No wonder I was glad to get away.
Mind you, I waited till Len said the word.
I didn't want the blame if things went wrong.     150
I was glad though, no end, when we moved out,
And I looked to be happy, and I was,
As I said, for a while—but I don't know!
Somehow the change wore out like a prescription.
And there's more to it than just window views     155
And living by a lake. I'm past such help
Unless Len took the notion, which he won't,
And I won't ask him—it's not sure enough.
I s'pose I've got to go the road I'm going:
Other folks have to, and why shouldn't I?     160
I almost think if I could do like you,
Drop everything and live out on the ground—
But it might be, come night, I shouldn't like it,
Or a long rain. I should soon get enough,
And be glad of a good roof overhead.     165
I've lain awake thinking of you, I'll warrant,
More than you have yourself, some of these nights.
The wonder was the tents weren't snatched away

> From over you as you lay in your beds.
> I haven't courage for a risk like that.                    170
> Bless you, of course you're keeping me from work,
> But the thing of it is, I need to *be* kept.
> There's work enough to do—there's always that;
> But behind's behind. The worst that you can do
> Is set me back a little more behind.                       175
> I shan't catch up in this world, anyway.
> I'd *rather* you'd not go unless you must.

The title of this poem refers to a passage in Genesis 9 where Noah curses Canaan, son of Ham, because Ham had seen "his father's nakedness" and told his brothers. In cursing Canaan, Noah declares he will become "a servant of servants"—specifically of Japheth and Shem, Ham's brothers. The speaker of the poem is not a servant, strictly speaking, though she feels like one, with "a houseful of hungry men to feed." These men are, it transpires, her husband's hired men, so that in a sense she does serve servants. The reference to Ham and Canaan at once introduces the topic of nakedness, and with it sexuality, which loom large in the background of this "servant to servants."

Like most dramatic monologues, this poem has an interlocutor, a camper on the "Servant's" land, as we learn from the first two lines. At first it is not clear whether the speaker is addressing one person or more than one; lines 168–69, with their mention of beds and tents in the plural, imply that there is definitely more than one camper, but apparently only one of them has come to the "Servant's" door, since she says "yourself," rather than "yourselves" in line 167. The campers are botanists; they have read about the area in a book about ferns and have presumably come on this camping trip to study them. These lines (33–35) set the scene of the poem as Lake Willoughby, a remote part of northern Vermont. The speaker obviously feels that it is too remote; she seems slightly surprised that the campers like the area and somewhat reluctant to agree with them: "I can see how you might. But I don't know! / It would be different if more people came." This explains why she is so glad to have the campers on the land, as she says in line 1, and why she had looked forward to visiting them. She starts to explain that she has not yet had time for this, but breaks off to remark "It seems to me / I can't express my feelings"—which represents a big leap from simply excusing herself for having been too busy to visit them. An inability to express feelings is common to many of Frost's dramatic speakers. Our impression of overreaction and unbalance is corroborated a few lines later by the "Servant's" comment that "It's got so I don't even know for sure / Whether I *am* glad, sorry, or anything," and the ominous phrase that she is "all gone wrong" (l. 15). Another hint that all is not well with her comes in lines 46–47, when she explains that Len, her husband, "thinks I'll be all right / With doctoring"; finally we realize that she has already spent some time in the State Asylum (l. 91) and worries about a recurrence of insanity.

From what we learn of the woman's background, it is not surprising if her mind is unbalanced. In the middle section of the poem she tells her auditor the story of her uncle who "went mad quite young," probably because of an unhappy love affair, since "all he talked about was love" (ll. 108–10). Because he was violent, the family built a cage for him, like a "beast's stall," with straw for a bed since he destroyed anything else; he also insisted on taking off all his clothes. The theme of nakedness from Genesis appears here, and also that of sexuality, for the uncle used to shout out in the night about "love things." The "Servant's" poor mother had to listen to this when she came as a bride to the farm. The speaker herself did not hear it, since she never actually saw her uncle; somehow, the family "found a way to put a stop to it," in the speaker's ominous phrase (l. 139)—a hint perhaps at castration, or even murder. The understatement of this line is reminiscent of the Duke of Ferrara's "Then all smiles stopped together" in Browning's "My Last Duchess." But though the "Servant" never saw her uncle, this story, and especially the thought of her mother's plight ("That was what marrying father meant to her"), obviously preyed on her mind. Sexuality is associated for her with madness and bestiality, and she links herself with her uncle: she used to say, half-joking, "'It's time I took my turn upstairs in jail,'" and she often thinks of the "smooth hickory bars." Eventually, her husband suggested moving away, perhaps after the breakdown that sent her to the State Asylum—a stay that she found preferable to her uncle's home treatment (ll. 97–103).

For a while the speaker was happy in the new location by Lake Willoughby, but it soon became apparent, at least to her, that there was more to it "than just window views / And living by a lake" (ll. 155–56). Her problems lie deeper, and the lake itself represents more to her than "just window views." She has already described how she would "step outdoors and take the water dazzle / A sunny morning, or take the rising wind / About my face and body and through my wrapper" (ll. 27–29). The emphasis here on "taking," and on feeling the wind through her wrapper, suggests a very sensual enjoyment of the weather and conveys a desire for exposure reminiscent of the uncle who removed his clothes. This idea is taken up again at the end of the poem when the speaker admits she has lain awake sometimes at night when the weather was bad, worrying whether "the tents weren't snatched away / From over you as you lay in your beds."

These hints seem to suggest, on the part of the speaker, a simultaneous apprehension and attraction in matters concerning nakedness and sexuality. Given her background and her obvious fascination with the story of her uncle, the poem implies that her mental problems are related to sexuality—though she seems unaware of this, claiming only to need more rest (l. 49). Once again we find the dramatic monologue being used, as by Browning in "The Bishop Orders His Tomb at Saint Praxed's Church," to reveal more about the protagonist than he knows about himself, or she knows about herself.

The "Servant's" husband does not help her much. He apparently made the move to Lake Willoughby for her sake, though he may have wished to move away from people who knew she had spent time in the asylum, being ashamed of the connection. In any case, he is too insensitive to understand the depth of her obsession or appreciate the fragility of her mental state. An inveterate optimist and believer in hard work, Len is sure she will pull through (ll. 55–56). The speaker puts another connotation on these words when she adds "I can see no way out but through," using "through" here not only in the sense of getting through a difficulty but also to mean "over," "finished"—implying that one way "out" will be when her own life is over; "and then they'll be convinced," she concludes, with childish triumph: people like Len will not be convinced except by physical proof.

The speaker's reference to her own possible death here illuminates her earlier curious description of the lake as "so long and narrow, / Like a deep piece of some old running river / Cut short off at both ends" (ll. 19–21). Perhaps this is how she views her own life—her childhood "Cut short off" because of her uncle's ravings, and her present life to be "Cut short off" by either death or madness. Also, her reference a few lines later to storms on the lake can be taken to symbolize the subdued violence of her stormy inner life: "And all our storms come up toward the house, / Drawing the slow waves whiter and whiter and whiter." The rhythm of this last line, the alliteration of *w* and persistent repetition of "whiter" convey a sense of feverish excitement—and an ominous movement toward obliterating blankness.

Len is unaware of the storms that threaten his wife's sanity. He is too optimistic to admit that she still has mental difficulties, and his down-to-earth view of life makes him insensitive to problems he would no doubt consider fanciful. The speaker herself is amazed that the campers have allowed ferns, "things more like feathers," to dictate their comings and goings. Len's work involves more practical matters such as real estate and highways (ll. 41 and 71–72). He might help his wife somewhat simply by paying more attention to her, but he seems more interested in his work than in his relationship with his wife, or in any manifestation of feeling. He is a hard worker, "But work ain't all," as she points out in one short but significant phrase. No doubt she would prefer him to work less and spend more time with her— or at least hire fewer men so that she would have less work (ll. 72–78). Her attitude toward the hired men is ambiguous: certainly she hates their behavior (ll. 74–77) and the extra work their presence entails; but she adds, "I'm not afraid of them, though, if they're not / Afraid of me. There's two can play at that. / I have my fancies: it runs in the family." This sentence leads straight into the story of her uncle's life, which tends to confirm that the "fancies" she mentions in relation to the hired men are sexual in nature.

The move to the lake has not cured her: "I'm past such help—" she declares, "Unless Len took the notion, which he won't, / And I won't ask him—it's not sure enough." Whatever "notion" she has in mind here—perhaps a return to the asylum for a while— she is quite sure the unimaginative Len will not suggest it or even think of it. Not that she blames him; on the contrary, in her self-deprecating way she defends his outlook; she is sure he wants the best for her (l. 60). The problem is that he does not know what the best would be. She concludes that she simply has to go on as before: "I s'pose I've got to go the road I'm going"— even if this road leads to death or insanity, as seems highly likely. She entertains briefly the fantasy of leaving home for a vagrant life of camping out, like her interlocutors, but quickly dismisses it because of the material discomforts involved (ll. 161–65).

By now her interlocutor clearly is anxious to escape from her depressing revelations. She would like to keep him (or her) longer ("I'd *rather* you'd not go unless you must"), and avoid returning to work, because she knows she needs the rest and she has enjoyed the opportunity to tell her story. Besides, even if she gets behind in her work it will make no difference. Her labors are of the type that always renew themselves ("Things . . . that just won't stay done") and, as she points out in a line that again seems to foretell her death, "I shan't catch up in this world, anyway" (l. 176).

A full-fledged dramatic monologue, this poem boasts a speaker who is certainly placed in a dramatic situation, since her sanity is at stake. All dramatic monologues have a narrative dimension, and that element is particularly strong here in the speaker's account of her family background. Our knowledge of her life is incomplete, but the details she gives contribute to the picture of a highly disturbed but lucid individual, remarkably aware of the danger she is in and clutching at any help or diversion within her grasp—here, the fortuitous presence of the unknown botanists. As in Browning's monologues, the speaker addresses her auditor periodically and makes comments that imply his response, for example: "How did you hear of it? . . . / In a book about ferns?" and "Bless you, of course you're keeping me from work," as the camper, anxious to get away, has no doubt politely inquired about her work.

The oral quality of the language is established in many ways. The poem is written in blank verse with a basic pattern of iambic pentameters. However, the frequent run-on lines, and the pauses at various points in mid-line, create a natural-sounding rhythm that disguises the basic iambic pattern. The rhythm is very loose, with many displaced stresses, as if to emphasize the rambling, disconnected nature of the speaker's thoughts. For example, the line "I can't express my feelings any more" may be a regular iambic pentameter, but most lines contain variations on this pattern, for example, "My hand (oh, I can lift it when I have to)." Line 6 has only eight syllables, the long pause in mid-line evidently accounting for the other two. Some lines have more than ten syllables ("It took my mind off doughnuts and soda-biscuit").

Other features of the poem suggest oral diction. There are exclamations such as "Listen to that!" or "Much they care!"; many questions also occur, which help to convey the impression of spoken discourse. The dash is used frequently as a way of suggesting the loose syntactical links characteristic of speech, especially hers ("Cruel—it sounds"). Sometimes the speaker uses incomplete sentences (e.g., ll. 156–58), or gives up on her train of thought with an "I don't know!" (ll. 4, 153); such interruptions not only suggest oral discourse but also betray the speaker's confused state of mind. Her habit of hopping from one subject of conversation to another could also be seen as a sign of psychic disjunction.

The speaker of "A Servant to Servants" is not characterized as fully as the protagonist of a Browning dramatic monologue, partly at least because the focus of interest is on her situation and mental state rather than on her personality. But since the main focus is on her state of mind, the dramatic monologue is an ideal vehicle for portraying it. The monologue enables her, with her lucid understanding of her own situation, to explain herself to a large extent, while unwittingly revealing that certain aspects of her situation escape her, such as the link between her mental instability and repressed sexuality.

There is a suggestion—when the speaker talks of standing by the lake allowing the wind to blow through her clothes, and when she fantasizes at the end about leading the life of the campers—that communion with nature might represent a liberating and healthy alternative to life with Len. An outdoor life could provide a means of escape from a house that has become a bastion of masculinity: the domain of the practical, down-to-earth Len, who does a man's work, "from sun to sun," and of his hired men, "great good-for-nothings, / Sprawling about the kitchen with their talk." Pitted against this authoritarian, masculine world, where there is little chance of survival for "things like feathers"—the delicate mechanisms of feeling—the Servant presents a pathetic figure. She has not learned to express her feelings fully; when she attempts to do so, in the speech that constitutes the poem, her interlocutor is a total outsider who would probably prefer not to listen; and she is married to a man who seems oblivious to the realm of emotion. As Stuart James remarks, this poem gives "an ugly and disturbing vision" of home life in a home that has become like a prison for the speaker.[4]

In a sense, the prison is in the speaker's own mind: the madness stemming from her memories of the "room within a room" built for her uncle has created its own "room" in her mind and threatens to invade it totally[5]; but the conditions of her present home life do nothing to alleviate the mental disturbance originating in her childhood. Richard Poirier suggests that this poem "is a frightening and pitiable dramatization of how a 'home,' deprived of emotional fulfillments of any kind, can prompt a woman to perverse and beautiful extremities."[6] Many of Frost's poems present a negative view of home life—often the struggle, as in "A Servant to Servants," between authoritarian or unfeeling men and obsessive women who have not fully learned the language of feeling and suffer both from the depth of their emotion and their inability to express it. Other such poems are "The Witch of Coos," "The Fear," and the superb "Home Burial." As Poirier says, "Frost is often at his best when 'home' is at its worst."

## Richard Howard

Richard Howard is a contemporary poet who has produced many volumes of poetry, including several collections of dramatic monologues, and is still writing dramatic monologues today. Born in 1929, he studied at Columbia and at the Sorbonne, and is well known for his translations of French poetry and of influential French theorists such as Roland Barthes. The art of poetic translation resembles the composition of dramatic monologues in that the author must reproduce the words of another in his own voice, as does a dramatic monologue.

Howard's collection of monologues *Untitled Subjects* won the Pulitzer Prize for 1970; *Findings* (1971) contains more dramatic monologues; subsequent collections include *Two-Part Inventions* (1974), *Fellow Feelings* (1976), *Misgivings* (1979), *Lining Up* (1983), and *Like Most Revelations* (1994). In many of these volumes Howard experiments in various ways with the dramatic monologue form. He has also written essays on poetry: *Alone With America: Essays on the Art of Poetry in the United States Since 1950*

(1969), and *Preferences* (1974)—a critical anthology of contemporary and earlier poets.

The poem we will examine, "A Pre-Raphaelite Ending, London," appears in *Untitled Subjects* (1969), a collection of dramatic monologues with different speakers, or subjects, whose identities are indicated only partially by the poems' titles, and more fully in notes at the beginning of the volume. The note concerning "A Pre-Raphaelite Ending" reads: "1915: The speaker is Mrs. William Morris, addressing her daughter May, a spinster in her late forties." It is also helpful, in reading this poem, to know that Jane Morris, née Burden, was loved by the pre-Raphaelite painter and poet Dante Gabriel Rossetti (1828–1882), the "Gabriel" she mentions. Most of the famous pictures from the latter half of Rossetti's career were painted with Jane as model.

This dramatic monologue presents a speaker, identified as Jane Morris, talking to an interlocutor, her daughter May, in a clearly defined dramatic situation, namely, shortly before her death. She is going through her papers—letters, drawings, and photographs—and handing them over to May. Hence the emphasis on "things" at the beginning and end of the poem: the word "things" is repeated three times in the first five lines, and the notion of possession is reinforced by the repetition of "have" in "the value things will come to have" and at the "rhyming" position in "things are what you have / left. And all you have." These things will survive Jane's death and are to be saved: "Save" is the first word of the poem, which also ends with a play on the word: "These are mine. Save them. / I have nothing save them."

The lines of the poem do not rhyme in the traditional sense, but there are some repetitions like those above (cf. also "gone" in ll. 7–8), and occasionally, rhymes at a distance, like "away / harm's way" or "sit / Is it" and "lot / not." The poem is divided into stanzas, though they flow together without spaces between them. Each stanza begins with a short line containing seven syllables with, usually, three stresses, for example, "Once the Zeppelins are gone," "Often Gabriel painted," and "was cold in his grave at last." The next three lines are slightly longer, generally comprising ten syllables with four stresses, and they are followed by two short lines of five syllables with two stresses each. The positioning of the stresses varies from line to line, which produces a varied rhythm resembling that of the speaking voice.

The many run-on lines contribute to an overall impression of oral diction, which is increased for the reader by the fact that only the initial words of sentences are capitalized, rather than the first word of each line. Nevertheless, as with all verse, the reader is aware of the tension between the phrasing of the sentences and the structure of the lines, with their fixed number of syllables and stresses. A similar tension is apparent in the poem's content: Jane tells her story freely, but only within the limits of a psychological restraint that prevents her from openly acknowledging Gabriel's love for her or hers for him.

The effect of the two short lines at the end of each stanza is to emphasize them, bringing out the dramatic content of lines like "These are mine. Save them. / I have nothing save them," or "he stifled the blood / Streaming from his mouth," or "They must be naked / drawings of me . . . ." Elsewhere, the short lines give the quality of a jingle to Gabriel's name for William: "Tops, the poetic / upholstery-man." ("Tops" or "Topsy" was Morris's nickname, borrowed from *Uncle Tom's Cabin,* adopted by all his close friends, and apparently inspired by his shock of curly hair.)

William Morris was a man of many talents. Known principally as a designer, he also did some painting, wrote poetry, and in the last decades of his life, wrote and made speeches in the Socialist cause. He designed furniture, glasswork, jewelry, carpets, printed fabrics and tapestries; and he founded firms that manufactured these items, as well as a printing press that produced beautiful books. In the poem, Jane refers to these interests when she says she will be gone "out of this chair, this bed, this *furniture,*" and again at the end when she mentions her "gown, one / of his designs I had worn all those days." She seems to imply that William was too concerned with things at the expense of people; "Remember how / he loved to list the things he owned," she says in stanza 8, and toward the end of the poem "William's mind was set / on things more significant / than human lives, individual lives . . . ."

Morris was renowned for his bad temper, as Jane mentions in the poem (stanza 10). By all accounts he was also singularly lacking in personal charm. According to Stanley Weintraub's biography of the four Rossettis, Morris, to Jane, was "a loud bore whose enthusiasms she tolerated by retreating into silence and her embroidery."[7] In the poem, she refers to William's Socialist friends as a "loud group of yellowing rowdies / who called them-

selves 'communists.'" She finds some letters he sent her when he
was away from them—and from her—in Iceland. (Morris had
always been interested in the Scandinavian epic, had taught
himself Icelandic, and visited Iceland.) Indeed, she evidently preferred to read his letters than to hear his voice, for "he wrote,
always, / lovely letters—if / you did not have to hear him / say
the words, as if he were breaking off / bones, throwing them
aside . . . ."

Morris, Rossetti, and Jane Burden had met in Oxford in 1857.
The two men, along with Edward Burne-Jones and other painter
friends, were decorating a hall in the Union of Oxford
University. They needed models for their mural paintings and
came across the seventeen-year-old Jane Burden, daughter, as
she says in the poem, of an "Oxford / livery-stable keeper."
Rossetti was attracted to her, at least aesthetically, but he was
already heavily involved with a young lady named Elizabeth
Siddal, whom he had known since 1850 and finally married in
1860 after many emotional upheavals. Meanwhile, Morris had
fallen in love with Jane; in Oxford he had painted her and written on the back of the picture, as Jane says in the poem, "I / can't
paint you but I love you" (Weintraub, 97). They were married in
1859.

In 1862 Elizabeth, who had been ill almost since Rossetti first
met her, took a (probably deliberate) overdose of the laudanum
she had used as a pain-killer. Rossetti felt guilt and remorse for a
long time after her death, but that did not prevent him, a few
years later, from falling in love with Jane Morris. She sat for him,
and by 1869 there were pictures of her all over his house. A sonnet in Rossetti's *The House of Life* entitled "The Portrait," possibly
celebrating one of his pictures of Jane, reads:

> Lo! it is done. Above the enthroning throat
> The mouth's mould testifies of voice and kiss
> The shadowed eyes remember and foresee.
> Her face is made her shrine. Let all men note
> That in all years (O Love, thy gift is this!)
> They that would look on her must come to me.

In July 1869 Rossetti wrote the letter from which Jane quotes
in Howard's poem (stanza 7): "Absence from your sight is what I
have long been used to; and no absence can ever make me so far

from you again as your presence did for years. For this long inconceivable change, you know now what my thanks must be."[8] In the poem, Jane conflates this letter with another, dated February 1870, where Gabriel declares: "No one else seems alive at all to me now, and places that are empty of you are empty of all life" (*Correspondence*, 34). This letter goes on to say: "You are the noblest and dearest thing that the world has had to show me"; in 1878 he still talks of his feeling for her as being "far deeper . . . than I have entertained towards any other living creature at any time of my life. Would that circumstances had given me the power to prove this" (*Correspondence*, 68).

Jane and Gabriel conducted a voluminous correspondence. In one letter Jane states that "to wade through a drawer-full of your letters would be the work of a day for me" (*Correspondence*, 83). However, Jane eventually destroyed many of his letters, and instructed Gabriel to do likewise, so that little or no evidence remains of their correspondence during the crucial years of 1870 to 1877.[9] However, she kept his letters from before and after that period, and they have been published, as well as a few of Jane's. Some of Gabriel's reveal his love for Jane, as we have seen; hers, from 1878 to 1881, are much more discreet; in any case her love had cooled by then to affection and sympathy.

In the poem Jane says, of Gabriel's love for her, that her husband William "knew of it, / but trusted." Certainly he knew of it: in the summer of 1871 and again for several months from 1872 to 1874, Jane and Gabriel lived together, with Jane's young daughters Jenny and May, at Kelmscott Manor, a country-house leased jointly by Rossetti and Morris. The house is located west of Oxford, just inside the Gloucestershire border, and the village of Kelmscott boasts a hall dedicated to the memory of William Morris. Having signed the lease on the house in 1871, Morris left for Iceland, and on his return remained in London, Jane leaving Kelmscott periodically to visit him. She also returned to London for the winter, when the river often flooded the fields around Kelmscott Manor.

While they were together at Kelmscott in the summer of 1871, Gabriel painted Jane and wrote sonnets; they went for long walks and played with Jane's daughters and with the dogs Gabriel acquired[10]—whereas Morris, as Jane says (stanza 4), "was not fond of animals." One of the sonnets written at this time, "The Lovers' Walk," evokes "two souls softly spann'd / With one o'erarching heaven of smiles and sighs," and describes how their "bodies lean unto / Each other's visible sweetness amorously." In the following year, 1872, Rossetti suffered a severe mental breakdown, from which he was to recover, though never fully. He convalesced at Kelmscott in the autumn, remaining there for eighteen months, during which time Jane again came to join him for long periods. Whether they were technically lovers is not known: Jane is said to have stated, later in her life, that she had "never quite given herself" to Gabriel (Marsh, 197).

In the poem, Jane mentions the phenomenon of the floods at Kelmscott in connection with Ruskin's visit to her there (stanza 14): "He [Ruskin] came to Kelmscott / —the meadows flooded / that year, and the noise / of water filled the air." Ruskin was an influential critic and an admirer of pre-Raphaelite art, including Rossetti's. The purpose of his visit to Jane in the poem was to give her some drawings —"naked / drawings," she supposes, of herself, done by Rossetti, which Ruskin must have bought after Rossetti's death, "to keep the world and William / from seeing," but which he could not bring himself to burn. Ruskin said that no one must see these drawings until after Jane's death, least of all William of course, who waited but died first (in 1896); May, too, must wait for her mother's death (stanza 14). Ruskin had also brought to Kelmscott a remedy for Jane's ailments in the form of "ivory dust / to be made into a jelly," a concoction he had also offered back in 1855 to Elizabeth Siddal (Weintraub, 83).

In the same section of the poem (stanza 22) Jane compares herself to "Mariana / in the moated grange" who is the deserted heroine of Tennyson's poem "Mariana," awaiting her lover who does not come—as well as being a girl in *Measure for Measure* (Tennyson's source for the character) wrongly accused of infidelity to her fiancé. Tennyson's poem was very popular in the late 19th century, and mention of it helps to place Jane in her time, like the reference to Ruskin. The setting of "A Pre-Raphaelite Ending" is London, according to the title. Jane's daughter May had a house in Hammersmith, southwest of central London. Perhaps this is where Jane is "kept . . . out of harm's way," according to her own words in the poem. She is worried, she says, about the Zeppelins—the airships invented by the German Baron Von Zeppelin, first flown in 1900, and used in World War I to bomb London. Howard has set the poem in 1915, when the Zeppelins were used, though Jane died (in Bath, at the age of 75) early in 1914, well before the outbreak of war (Marsh, 269). Nevertheless, the reference to Zeppelins situates the poem in both time and place.

Another 19th-century figure mentioned in the poem is Dodgson. Charles Dodgson's pseudonym was Lewis Carroll; he took photographs of Jane, from which Rossetti painted, as Jane says, "when he could not see me" (stanza 6). Many of Rossetti's surviving letters to Jane arrange times for her to come and sit for pictures (e.g., *Correspondence*, 1, 150); in this case, in the poem, Jane quotes from one of Gabriel's notes: "Dearest Janey, / Dodgson will he here tomorrow at noon, / do come as early as you can manage."

Having reflected on Gabriel's letters, William's idiosyncrasies ("You know what his rages were—"), and Ruskin's visit with the drawings, Jane's meditations take a more philosophical turn:

> It was an abyss then, an imbroglio
> then and after. The reciprocal
> life of "well persons"
> grew impossible.

In lines with an Eliotic ring she muses that

> Moments come when the pattern
> is laid before us, plain. And then we know
> the limitations, accidentally
> repeated, are the stuff of life. They will
> return again, for
> they are just . . . ourselves.

(The references to the "pattern" and the "stuff" of life recall Morris's work as a designer of fabrics.) The pessimistic tone of these lines culminates in the anguish of the following ones;

> Then we know that this and none
> other will be our life. And so begins
> a long decay—we die from day to dream,
> and common speech we answer with a scream.

The uncharacteristically blatant rhyme underscores the pain lying behind her memories, which leads Jane to say hurriedly "Put those things aside" and turn to William's "lovely letters" and to thoughts of him. The poem ends with her repeated injunction to her daughter to "save it all," for "the rest of the things are mere images, / not medieval"—like the subjects of so much pre-Raphaelite art—but "only middle-aged" and therefore lacking in excitement, "wonderful but dead."

As in a Browning monologue, the speaker of "A Pre-Raphaelite Ending, London" manages, in the natural course of conversation, to evoke a good part of her life history, in particular her relationship with two men and, through them, with other members of the Pre-Raphaelite movement. The tone of the poem is conversational, though without the colloquialisms and interjections typical of Browning. The syntax is loose like that of oral speech ("'Jane, / I wegwet,' he said—he could not pronounce / his r's, odd in a man named Ruskin"), and the speaker tends to hop from one topic to another, for example, from thoughts of her illness, to Ruskin (via his phrase "*Tragic health*") and his visit to Kelmscott, when the meadows were flooded, to hand her the pictures—but not before commenting on the butterfly that settled on her shoulder or picking some cress growing by the path. The speaker is placed in a specific setting and in a specific dramatic context as, at the approach of death, she anticipates the revelation of her private affairs to the world through the letters, photographs, and drawings she has accumulated over the course of an eventful life.

In *Untitled Subjects* Richard Howard pays tribute to his predecessors in the art of dramatic monologue, Tennyson and Browning: the volume is dedicated indirectly to Browning, "the great poet of otherness"; and it contains a poem about Tennyson set at Freshwater, Tennyson's residence on the Isle of Wight. Another of Howard's collections, *Findings* (1971), includes "November, 1889," a long and fascinating dramatic monologue purportedly spoken by Browning in the last days of his life and addressed to his son Pen and daughter-in-law Fanny. Monologues and dialogues also may be found in *Two-Part Inventions* (1974). *Fellow Feelings* (1976) contains monologues, often addressed *to* famous figures rather than spoken by them. Similarly, in *Lining Up* (1984) many poems are addressed, in the second person, to various painters, musicians, and writers, such as Delacroix, Millet, Corot, Verdi, Berlioz, and Gérard de Nerval.

The dramatic monologue may never again know the vogue it enjoyed in the late 19th century. One reason for its popularity then—apart from the fact that it was perceived as a new and therefore exciting form—was unquestionably the opportunity it provided to explore the speaker's psychology and the motivation behind his discourse. Another feature of the dramatic monologue may explain its appeal in the 19th century: because it presents a character's speech (or thoughts), it allows the poet—if he so wishes—to employ an oral diction that in the Victorian era was still unusual in poetry. Poetic language was restricted generally to the "good English" decried by Pound. In the 20th century, it has become perfectly acceptable for any poetry to be written in an oral idiom, whether the voice of the poem belongs to an identified speaker, as in a dramatic monologue, or not. Consequently, a poet who wishes to use colloquial diction no longer needs to turn to the dramatic monologue in order to justify such discourse. This may be one reason why it has diminished somewhat in popularity.

Nevertheless, as this brief (and certainly not exhaustive) survey of 20th-century examples shows, the dramatic monologue has continued to attract many poets, especially American ones, including some of the most outstanding. Poets with a strong lyric bent tend to ignore it. Certain poets—Eliot, Pound, Robert Lowell—wrote dramatic monologues early in their careers but later adopted a different kind of poetic persona. Some, like Frost, Jarrell, and Robert Lowell, interspersed dramatic monologues with other poems, either more lyrical, or even more dramatic, like Frost's many poems that are made up primarily of dialogue. And in Richard Howard we have an example of a contemporary poet whose work consists largely of dramatic monologues, though he rings many changes on the basic pattern of the genre. In the century that has passed since the deaths of Browning and Tennyson, the dramatic monologue has remained a popular form among poets who, for whatever reason, wish to speak through the voice of another.

# Notes and References

### Chapter One

1. Benjamin Fuson, *Browning and His English Predecessors in the Dramatic Monolog* (Iowa City: State University of Iowa Press, 1948), 15–21, hereafter cited in text; Ina B. Sessions, "The Dramatic Monologue," *Publications of the Modern Language Association of America (PMLA)* 62 (1947), 503–16.

2. Robert Langbaum, *The Poetry of Experience: The Dramatic Monologue in Modern Literary Tradition* (1957; rpt. Chicago and London: University of Chicago Press, 1985), 76–78, hereafter cited in text.

3. Frances Carleton, *The Dramatic Monologue: Vox Humana* (Salzburg: Salzburg University Press, 1977), 2; Roma A. King, Jr., *The Focusing Artifice* (Athens: Ohio University Press, 1968), 65; Donald S. Hair, *Browning's Experiments With Genre* (Toronto: University of Toronto Press, 1972), 100; Park Honan, *Browning's Characters* (New Haven: Yale University Press, 1961), 123.

4. Ekbert Faas, *Retreat Into the Mind: Victorian Poetry and the Rise of Psychiatry* (Princeton, NJ: Princeton University Press, 1988), 94, hereafter cited in text. On the question of the persona, see Robert C. Elliott, *The Literary Persona* (Chicago and London: Chicago University Press, 1982), hereafter cited in text.

5. Reuben Brower, "The Speaking Voice," in *Approaches to the Poem,* ed. John O. Perry (San Francisco: Chandler, 1965), 259;

John Crowe Ransom, *The World's Body* (New York: Scribner's, 1938), 250.

6. Sharon Cameron, *Lyric Time: Dickinson and the Limits of Genre* (Baltimore and London: Johns Hopkins University Press, 1979), 208, hereafter cited in text.

7. William Elford Rogers, *The Three Genres and the Interpretation of Lyric* (Princeton, NJ: Princeton University Press, 1983), 82, hereafter cited in text.

8. Kate Hamburger, *The Logic of Literature*, trans. Marilynn J. Rose, 2nd rev. ed. (Bloomington: Indiana University Press, 1973), 310, hereafter cited in text.

9. Loy D. Martin, *Browning's Dramatic Monologues and the Post-Romantic Subject* (Baltimore and London: Johns Hopkins University Press, 1985), 112, hereafter cited in text; Ralph W. Rader, "The Dramatic Monologue and Related Lyric Forms," *Critical Inquiry*, 3 (1976), 133, hereafter cited in text; Alan Sinfield, *Dramatic Monologue* (London: Methuen, 1977), 25, hereafter cited in text.

10. M.M. Bakhtin, *The Dialogic Imagination* (Austin: University of Texas Press, 1981), 324 and 285–87 and 297.

11. Jonathan Culler, *The Pursuit of Signs: Semiotics, Literature, Deconstruction* (Ithaca, NY: Cornell University Press, 1981), 149.

12. K.W. Gransden, "The Uses of Personae," in *Browning's Mind and Art*, ed. Clarence Tracy (Edinburgh and London: Oliver and Boyd, 1968), 66; Douglas Bush, *Mythology and the Romantic Tradition in English Poetry* (New York: Pageant Books, 1957), 365.

13. Barbara Herrnstein Smith asserts the fictive nature of poetic utterance also, in "Poetry as Fiction," *New Literary History*, 2, no. 2 (Winter 1971), 259–81.

14. Ralph W. Rader, "Notes of Some Structural Varieties and Variations in Dramatic 'I' Poems and Their Theoretical Implications," *Victorian Poetry*, 22 (Summer 1984), 105, hereafter cited in text; and "The Dramatic Monologue and Related Lyric Forms," (see note 9 above), 140.

15. E. Warwick Slinn, *Browning and the Fictions of Identity* (Totowa, NJ: Barnes and Noble, 1982), 161, hereafter cited in text.

16. Roma A. King, Jr., *The Bow and the Lyre: The Art of Robert Browning* (Ann Arbor: University of Michigan Press, 1964), 145: "The first criterion by which to judge a Browning monologue is the effectiveness of its characterization." Park Honan approaches Browning's monologues specifically "in the light of [their] character-revealing effects" (see note 3 above), 5.

17. Herbert F. Tucker, Jr., *Browning's Beginnings* (Minneapolis: University of Minnesota Press, 1980), 9.

18. Lee Erikson, *Robert Browning: His Poetry and His Audiences* (Ithaca,NY, and London: Cornell University Press, 1984), 84.

19. Clyde de L. Ryals, "Browning's Irony," in *The Victorian Experience: The Poets*, ed. Richard A. Levine (Athens: Ohio University Press, 1982), 24.

20. A. Dwight Culler, "Monodrama and the Dramatic Monologue," *PMLA*, 90 (1975),366, hereafter cited in text.

21. Plato, *Republic* III, 393c, trans. G.M.A Greebe, rev. by C.D.C. Reeve (Indianapolis and Cambridge: Hackett, 1992), 69. In *The Republic*, III, 392d–394c, Plato distinguishes between i) the voice of the poet speaking for himself, as in "dithyrambs" (choral songs, i.e., lyric poetry), ii) the purely "imitated" voice of characters speaking in dialogue, as in tragedy, and iii) the voice of epic poetry, which contains the other two: basically the poet narrates in his own voice, but often he represents, or imitates, the voice of characters speaking in their own person. None of these categories really applies to the dramatic monologue, where we hear the voice of a character speaking while we remain aware of the poet's presence in the poem.

22. Carol T. Christ, *Victorian and Modern Poetics* (Chicago and London: University of Chicago Press, 1984), 19.

23. Philip Hobsbaum, "The Rise of the Dramatic Monologue," *Hudson Review*, 28 (1975–76), 227–45; see especially 229–34. Similarly, Michael Mason suggests that a contemporary tendency to appreciate poeticity rather than action in stage drama may have led to the popularity of the dramatic monologue. Cf. Michael Mason, "Browning and the Dramatic Monologue," in *Robert Browning*, ed. Isobel Armstrong (London: Bell, 1974), 231–52.

24. For these thoughts on Dante I am grateful to Rachel Jacoff of Wellesley College.

25. Randall Jarrell's translation, from the "New Poems" section of *The Complete Poems* (New York: Farrar, Straus and Giroux, 1969). Jarrell also translated Rilke's "The Widow's Song" and Mörike's "The Forsaken Girl." I am grateful to my colleague Jutta Arend for pointing out these German poems to me.

26. The poems "Cancion del pirata," "El mendigo," and "El verdugo" appear in José de Espronceda, *El diablo mundo, El estudiante de Salamanca, Poesia,* ed. Jaime Gil de Biedma (Madrid: El Libro de Bolsillo, 1980). I am grateful to Kathy Pollakowski of Tufts University for pointing out these Spanish poems to me.

27. Stanislaw Baranczak, *A Fugitive from Utopia: The Poetry of Zbigniew Herbert* (Cambridge, MA: Harvard University Press, 1987), 98. The poem "The Elegy of Fortinbras" appears in *Zbigniew Herbert: Selected Poems,* trans. Czeslaw Milosz and Peter Dale Scott (Harmondsworth, Middlesex, England: Penguin Books, 1968). "The Divine Claudius" and "Damastes (Also Known As Procrustes) Speaks" appear in *Report From the Besieged City and Other Poems by Zbigniew Herbert,* trans. John Carpenter and Bogdana Carpenter (New York: Ecco Press, 1985).

28. See Elisabeth A. Howe, *Stages of Self: The Dramatic Monologues of Laforgue, Mallarmé and Valéry* (Athens: Ohio University Press, 1990), chapters 4, 5.

29. *The Letters of Ezra Pound, 1907–1914,* ed. D.D. Paige (New York: Harcourt Brace, 1950), 48; Eliot's Introduction to Valéry's *The Art of Poetry,* trans. Denise Folliot (London: Routledge and Kegan Paul, 1958), xvi–xvii.

30. Gerald L. Bruns, *Modern Poetry and the Idea of Language* (New Haven, CT: Yale University Press, 1974), 258–59; Robert W. Greene, *Six French Poets of Our Time* (Princeton: Princeton University Press, 1979), 9.

## Chapter Two

1. One of the latest readings also suggests many further, potential readings; see Mark Edmundson, "The Academy Writes

Back," in *Wild Orchids and Trotsky,* ed. Mark Edmundson (New York: Penguin Books, 1993), 21–27.

2. John Ruskin, *Works,* ed. E.T. Cook and Alexander Wedderburn (London: George Allen, 1905), VI, 449.

3. Park Honan, *Browning's Characters: A Study in Poetic Technique* (New Haven, CT: Yale University Press, 1961), 190.

4. K.W. Gransden, "The Uses of Personae," in *Browning's Mind and Art,* ed. Clarence Tracy (Edinburgh and London: Oliver and Boyd, 1968), 66.

5. Herbert F. Tucker, "Dramatic Monologue and the Overhearing of Lyric," in *Lyric Poetry: Beyond New Criticism,* ed. Chavira Hosek and Patricia Parker (Ithaca, NY: Cornell University Press, 1985), 230, hereafter cited in text.

6. Clyde de L. Ryals, *Becoming Browning: The Poems and Plays of Robert Browning, 1833–1846* (Columbus: Ohio State University Press, 1983), 149, hereafter cited in text.

7. Robert Langbaum, *The Poetry of Experience: The Dramatic Monologue in Modern Literary Tradition* (New York: Random House, 1957), 94, hereafter cited in text.

8. Walter Bagehot, "Wordsworth, Tennyson, and Browning; or, Pure, Ornate, and Grotesque Art in English Poetry," *Literary Studies* (London: Longmans, 1898), II, 305–51. See also Isobel Armstrong, "Browning and the Grotesque Style," in *The Major Victorian Poets: Reconsiderations,* ed. Isobel Armstrong (London: Routledge and Kegan Paul, 1969), 93–123.

9. Eliot, unpublished lecture quoted in F.O. Matthiessen, *The Achievement of T.S. Eliot,* 2nd ed. (New York and London: Oxford University Press, 1947), p. 74; *The Letters of Ezra Pound, 1907–1914,* ed. D.D. Paige (New York: Harcourt Brace, 1950), p. 48.

10. Hallam Tennyson, *Alfred Lord Tennyson: A Memoir,* 2 vols., (London: Macmillan, 1897), I, 396, hereafter cited in text.

11. Robert Bernard Martin, *Tennyson: The Unquiet Heart* (Oxford: Clarendon Press, 1980), 72.

12. Linda K. Hughes, *The Manyfacèd Glass: Tennyson's Dramatic Monologues* (Athens: Ohio University Press, 1987), 110.

13. For discussion of Ulysses' "death-wish," see A. Dwight Culler, *The Poetry of Tennyson* (New Haven, CT, and London: Yale University Press, 1977), 97; Elaine Jordan, *Alfred Tennyson* (Cambridge University Press, 1988), 70, hereafter cited in text; James R. Kincaid, *Tennyson's Major Poems: The Comic and Ironic Patterns* (New Haven, CT, and London: Yale University Press, 1975), p. 42; Alastair W. Thomson, *The Poetry of Tennyson* (London: Routledge and Kegan Paul, 1986), 66.

14. For discussion of Ulysses' personality and motivation, see Culler, *The Poetry of Tennyson*, pp. 95–96; Kincaid, *Tennyson's Major Poems*, 43–45 (see note 13); Robert Pattison, *Tennyson and Tradition* (Cambridge, MA: Harvard University Press, 1979), 84–85, hereafter cited in text; Thomson, *The Poetry of Tennyson*, 68–69 (see note 13); Linda K. Hughes, "Dramatis and Private Personae: 'Ulysses' Revisited," *Victorian Poetry*, 17 (1979), 192–203; W. David Shaw, *Tennyson's Style*, (Ithaca, NY: Cornell University Press, 1976), 85–86 (see note 17).

15. Daniel A. Harris, *Tennyson and Personification: The Rhetoric of "Tithonus"* (Ann Arbor, Michigan: UMI Research Press, 1986), 21.

16. The expression "withered immortality" is from a poem of Tennyson's youth entitled "The Grasshopper," which refers to Tithon. As contemporary readers of Tennyson would know, the gods did eventually, according to the Greek myth, take pity on Tithonus and turned him into a grasshopper—a withered-looking creature who chirps eternally; but in our poem Tithonus is unaware that this is to be his fate.

17. W. David Shaw, "Tennyson's 'Tithonus' and the Problem of Mortality," *Philological Quarterly*, 52 (1973), 276. Shaw discusses this question further in his *Tennyson's Style*, 89–91 (see note 14).

18. For a discussion of Bagehot's comments on Tennyson's "ornate" style, see W. David Shaw, *Tennyson's Style*, 38–41 (see note 14).

19. Many critics assume that Eos leaves Tithonus in the course of the poem (around line 45), and that the rest of the poem is a soliloquy. I am not convinced of this (the present tenses of

lines 32–42 could refer in a general sense to what happens every day rather than to what is happening "now" before Tithonus' eyes); however, in line 75, "these empty courts" does suggest she has left. If the second part of the poem *is* a soliloquy with "thou" representing an apostrophe to a now-absent Dawn who was present in lines 1–45, it just goes to show there is nothing to prevent a dramatic monologue from being a soliloquy: there is no alteration in form between lines 1–45 and 46–76.

As for "Ulysses," many critics see it as a soliloquy as far as line 33 when Ulysses turns to Telemachus; or as far as line 45 when he first addresses his mariners. But I see no reason why his mariners should not have been present from the beginning, and the whole poem addressed to them.

20. Alan Sinfield, *Alfred Tennyson* (Oxford: Blackwell, 1986), 86.

21. Douglas Bush, *Mythology and the Romantic Tradition in English Poetry* (Cambridge, MA: Harvard University Press, 1969), 197.

22. See the Appendix to Ekbert Faas, *Retreat Into the Mind: Victorian Poetry and the Rise of Psychiatry* (Princeton, NJ: Princeton University Press, 1988), 210–15. The Appendix is entitled "Practitioners of the Dramatic Monologue among Minor Victorian Poets" and lists scores of individual poems by title.

## Chapter Three

1. T.S. Eliot, "The Three Voices of Poetry," in *On Poetry and Poets* (New York: Noonday Press, 1961), 103–04.

2. Michael Bernstein, *Ezra Pound and the Modern Verse Epic: The Tale of the Tribe* (Princeton, NJ: Princeton University Press, 1980), 164.

3. Ezra Pound, *Literary Essays,* ed. T.S. Eliot (London: Faber and Faber, 1954), 419.

4. Letter of 1916 to Iris Barry, in *The Letters of Ezra Pound 1907–1941,* ed. D.D. Paige (New York: Harcourt Brace, 1950), 90.

5. Ezra Pound, *Selected Prose 1909–1965,* ed. William Cookson (New York: New Directions, 1973), 462.

6. Letter of 1915 to Harriet Monroe, *Letters*, 48–49.

7. Thomas H. Jackson, *The Early Poetry of Ezra Pound* (Cambridge, MA: Harvard University Press, 1968), 4.

8. Ezra Pound, "Vorticism" in *Gaudier-Brzeska: A Memoir* (New York: New Directions, 1960), 85.

9. Letter of 1908 to William Carlos Williams, *Letters*, 3–4.

10. Unpublished lecture quoted in F.O. Matthiessen, *The Achievement of T.S. Eliot: An Essay on the Nature of Poetry*, 3rd ed. (New York and London: Oxford University Press, 1958), 74.

11. Carol T. Christ, *Victorian and Modern Poetics* (Chicago: University of Chicago Press, 1986), 3, hereafter cited in text.

12. Peter Ackroyd, *T.S. Eliot* (London: Hamish Hamilton, 1985), 164–65, hereafter cited in text.

13. Philip R. Headings, *T.S. Eliot* (Boston: Twayne, 1964), 172.

14. *The Diary of Virginia Woolf*, Vol. 2, ed. Anne Oliver Bell (New York: Harcourt Brace, 1978), 68.

15. See Lyndall Gordon, *Eliot's Early Years*, (Oxford and New York: Oxford University Press, 1977), 26.

16. Hugh Kenner, *The Invisible Poet* (New York: McDowell, Obolensky, 1959), 30, hereafter cited in text.

17. John T. Mayer, *T.S. Eliot's Silent Voices* (Oxford and New York: Oxford University Press, 1989), 11.

18. T.S. Eliot, *Selected Essays* (New York, Harcourt Brace, 1950), 124–25, hereafter cited in text.

19. Wayne C. Booth, *The Rhetoric of Fiction* (Chicago: University of Chicago Press, 1961), 163.

20. M.M. Bakhtin, *The Dialogic Imagination: Four Essays*, ed. Michael Holquist, trans. Caryl Emerson and Michael Holquist (Austin: University of Texas Press, 1981), 324.

21. See Eliot's Introduction to Ezra Pound's *Selected Poems* (London: Faber and Gwyer, 1928), viii.

22. George T. Wright, *The Poet in the Poem: The Personae of Eliot, Yeats and Pound* (Berkeley and Los Angeles: University of California Press, 1962), 62.

23. Michael Bernstein, *Ezra Pound and the Modern Verse Epic: The Tale of the Tribe* (Princeton, NJ: Princeton University Press, 1980), 31, 76.

24. T.S. Eliot, "The Music of Poetry," in *On Poetry and Poets* (New York: Noonday Press, 1969), 31.

25. See Eliot's Introduction to Paul Valéry's *The Art of Poetry* (1958; rpt. New York: Vintage Press, 1961), xvi–xvii.

26. For a discussion of this question, see Ronald Bush, *T.S. Eliot: A Study in Character and Style* (Oxford and New York: Oxford University Press, 1983), especially 44–47.

Chapter Four

1. *The Poetry of Robert Frost*, ed. Edward Connery Lathem (New York: Holt, Rinehart and Winston, 1969), ix.

2. Frost's statement appears as the first sentence of his Preface to *A Way Out*, reprinted in *Selected Prose of Robert Frost*, ed. Hyde Cox and Edward Connery Lathem (New York, Chicago, San Francisco: Holt, Rinehart and Winston, 1966), 13. Eliot's question appears in "A Dialogue on Dramatic Poetry" in *Selected Essays, 1917–1932* (New York: Harcourt Brace, 1950), 38.

3. *Interviews With Robert Frost*, ed. Edward Connery Lathem (New York, Chicago, San Francisco: Holt, Rinehart and Winston, 1966), 257.

4. Stuart B. James, "The Home's Tyranny: Robert Frost's 'A Servant to Servants' and Andrew Wyeth's 'Christina's World,'" *South Dakota Review* I, no. 2 (1964), 4.

5. See Frank Lentricchia, *Robert Frost: Modern Poetics and the Landscapes of Self* (Durham, NC: Duke University Press, 1975), 68.

6. Richard Poirier, *Robert Frost: The Work of Knowing* (Stanford, CA: Stanford University Press,1977), 116. The quote that follows this note number is from 111.

7. Stanley Weintraub, *Four Rossettis: A Victorian Biography* (London: W.H. Allen, 1978), 156, hereafter cited in text.

8. *Dante Gabriel Rossetti and Jane Morris: Their Correspondence*, ed. John Bryson and Janet Camp Troxell (Oxford: Clarendon Press, 1976), 11.

9. Jan Marsh, *Jane and May Morris: A Biographical Story 1839–1938* (London and New York: Pandora, 1986), 131, hereafter cited in text.

10. Brian and Judy Dobbs, *Dante Gabriel Rossetti: An Alien Victorian* (London: Macdonald and Jane's, 1977), 200.

# Bibliographical Essay

This survey includes works on the dramatic monologue in general and books on the individual poets discussed in the foregoing chapters. The volume of critical studies of poets such as Browning, Tennyson, and Eliot is overwhelming: I have therefore selected mainly works that treat these poets specifically as authors of dramatic monologues, excluding, for example, studies of Pound's *Cantos* or Eliot's *Four Quartets*.

## Works on the Dramatic Monologue or on Related Topics

Histories of poetry, such as Roy Harvey Pearce's *The Continuity of American Poetry* (Princeton: Princeton University Press, 1961) or Hyatt Waggoner's *American Poets From the Puritans to the Present* (Baton Rouge: Louisiana State University Press, 1984) often tend to ignore the dramatic monologue, avoiding the term altogether, or they refer to the dramatic monologue in passing, but without defining it, like David Perkins in *A History of Modern Poetry: From the 1890s to the High Modernist Mode* (Cambridge, MA: Belknap Press of Harvard University Press, 1976); Stephen Gurney in *British Poetry of the Nineteenth Century* (New York: Twayne, 1993); John Garrett in *British Poetry Since the Sixteenth Century: A Student's Guide* (London: Macmillan, 1986); various contributors to *The Columbia History of American Poetry*, ed. Jay Parini (New

York: Columbia University Press, 1993), and *The Columbia History of British Poetry*, ed. Carl Woodring (New York: Columbia University Press, 1994). Obviously, the huge scope of such histories of poetry precludes detailed attention to any individual genre.

Studies of Victorian poetry usually refer to the dramatic monologue, since this was the period in which it flourished, but again there is often little attempt at definition. E.D.H. Johnson's main concern in *The Alien Vision of Victorian Poetry: Sources of the Poetic Imagination in Tennyson, Browning, and Arnold* (Hamden, CT: Anchor Books, 1963) is to examine the relationship of these poets to society in an increasingly materialist age. He mentions the dramatic monologue with respect to Browning, but only in passing. Bernard Richards' *English Poetry of the Victorian Period 1830–1890* (London and New York: Longman, 1988) emphasizes aspects of Victorian poetry such as diction, versification, imagery, and genre, as opposed to individual poets. Although he mentions the dramatic monologue as the "most significant generic innovation in the poetry of the century," he gives little in the way of definition beyond interest in character and incident, and specificity of context. He quotes very few examples of dramatic monologues (e.g., "Saint Simeon Stylites" and *The Ring and the Book*).

Given the popularity of the dramatic monologue in the Victorian era, it is ironic that a book that helped spark recent interest in the genre sets out to prove that the Victorians were not the first to produce the form. Benjamin Fuson, in *Browning and His English Predecessors in the Dramatic Monolog* (Iowa City: State University of Iowa Press, 1948), offers a definition of the dramatic monologue and shows that many poems were written in this form, or approximations of it, before "Porphyria's Lover" and "St. Simeon Stylites." Subsequently, Robert Langbaum published his seminal study entitled *The Poetry of Experience: The Dramatic Monologue in Modern Literary Tradition* (London: Chatto and Windus, 1957), which has been followed by a proliferation of works on the dramatic monologue or on specific poets as writers of dramatic monologues. Langbaum relates the dramatic monologue to the Romantic lyric, seeing it as an attempt to enter sympathetically into the subjective experience of others. The dramatic monologue is therefore a "poetry of experience" in which the reader's sympathy for the speaker outweighs any moral judgment. This view has been contested, but the book remains valuable, and influential. Hazard Adams, in *The Contexts of Poetry* (London: Methuen, 1965), includes a chapter entitled "Dramatic Monologue: Drama into Character," in which, like Langbaum, he sees the dramatic monologue as "an outgrowth of romantic subjectivity" (p. 145)—though he lays more stress on moral judgment than on sympathy in assessing characters like the Duke in "My Last Duchess" or the speaker of "Soliloquy of the Spanish Cloister." Concentrating on the dramatic monologue's capacity for revealing character, he contrasts it with soliloquy in stage drama, which also furthers the action of the play.

Many other books and articles try to elucidate the question of the dramatic monologue's origins. Michael Mason's article "Browning and the Dramatic Monologue" in *Robert Browning*, ed. Isobel Armstrong (London: Bell, 1974), attempts to redefine the dramatic monologue and also to understand how Browning came to this form. He investigates a contemporary preference for "poeticity" rather than action in (stage) drama, which may well have created a suitable climate for the development of the dramatic monologue. Similarly, Philip Hobsbaum regards the Victorian dramatic monologue as arising from stage monologues, and in particular from a tendency to value soliloquies above action in the theater ("The Rise of the Dramatic Monologue," *Hudson Review*, 28, 1975–1976). A. Dwight Culler sees a possible source of the dramatic monologue in the form known as the monodrama ("Monodrama and the Dramatic Monologue," *PMLA*, 90, 1975).

Ekbert Faas links the development of the dramatic monologue in Victorian times with the rise of psychiatry. In his book *Retreat Into the Mind: Victorian Poetry and the Rise of Psychiatry* (Princeton: Princeton University Press, 1988), he notes that writers of dramatic monologues were hailed in the 19th century as members of a "Psychological School of Poetry," and that the emergence of the dramatic monologue was simultaneous with a steadily increasing interest in human psychology. He points out that many speakers of 19th-century dramatic monologues are unbalanced or insane. His book makes a valuable and convincing contribution to the question of why the dramatic monologue genre flowered suddenly in the mid-19th century.

His comments on the impact of Shakespearean drama, with its linguistic realism and psychological insight, also are pertinent. The book discusses Browning's and Tennyson's adoption of the dramatic monologue form as well as the works of many other Victorian poets, notably Matthew Arnold and Swinburne. The Appendix contains a useful list of dramatic monologues by minor poets.

A short but reliable introduction to the dramatic monologue as a genre is Alan Sinfield's *Dramatic Monologue* (London: Methuen, 1977) in the *Critical Idiom* series. Sinfield discusses origins and characteristics of the form without, however, analyzing any individual poems. He refers mostly to Browning and Tennyson, with some mention of Eliot, Pound, and Robert Lowell. Frances Carleton's *The Dramatic Monologue: Vox Humana* (Salzburg: Salzburg Studies in English Literature, University of Salzburg, 1977) addresses the issues of voice and irony in the dramatic monologue; she also makes a distinction between dramatic monologue and interior monologue. Most of her discussion centers on Browning, though she mentions Arnold, Tennyson, Pound, Eliot, and Valéry.

Other books treat various aspects of the poetics of the dramatic monologue. Two articles by Ralph Rader discuss the question of voice in the dramatic monologue and its relation to the lyric: "The Dramatic Monologue and Related Lyric Forms," *Critical Inquiry*, 3 (1976), 131–51; and "Notes on Some Structural Varieties and Variations in Dramatic 'I' Poems and Their Theoretical Implications," *Victorian Poetry*, 22 (1984), 103–20. Rader attempts to set up a distinction between the "dramatic monologue proper" (certain poems of Browning), whose speaker is a simulated real person, and a form that he calls the "mask lyric," where the speaker is "an artificial person projected from the poet, a mask through which he speaks" ("The Dramatic Monologue . . ." p. 140). More convincingly, he analyzes the split inherent in the language of the dramatic monologue where the voices of the speaker and of the poet are heard simultaneously.

Differences between the dramatic monologue and the lyric are also explored by Herbert F. Tucker in his article "Dramatic Monologue and the Overhearing of Lyric," in *Lyric Poetry: Beyond New Criticism*, ed. Chaviva Hosek and Patricia Parker (Ithaca, NY: Cornell University Press, 1985). He offers a cogent and interesting discussion of the distinction between dramatic monologue and lyric poetry, of the mimetic impulse in Browning as opposed to the lyric impulse in Tennyson, and of the techniques and problems involved in the textual production of character.

Dorothy Mermin's *The Audience in the Poem: Five Victorian Poets* (New Brunswick, NJ: Rutgers University Press, 1983) analyzes Victorian poems with auditors (poems that are therefore representations of speech), many of which are dramatic monologues. This approach obviates the need to distinguish between dramatic monologue and lyric. She suggests that the focus of auditor poems is not to display character but to show "why, how, and to what effect the speaker speaks, and . . . various ways in which speech can be exploited, perverted, and misunderstood" (p. 47). The book examines auditor poems by Tennyson, Browning, Arnold, Clough, and Meredith.

The language of the dramatic monologue comes under scrutiny in Loy D. Martin's article "The Inside of Time: An Essay on the Dramatic Monologue" included in *Robert Browning: A Collection of Critical Essays*, a Spectrum Book edited by Harold Bloom and Adrienne Munich (Englewood Cliffs, NJ: Prentice-Hall, 1979). Martin studies the way the language of the dramatic monologue, specifically in its use of deictics and of certain verb forms, creates a sense of present time, viewed—as the poem's speaker views it—from the inside. He applies these observations to various monologues, in particular Browning's "My Last Duchess."

The Summer 1984 issue of *Victorian Poetry* (Vol. 22, no. 2) is devoted entirely to essays on the dramatic monologue, including the one by Ralph Rader mentioned above, an Introduction by Linda M. Shires, and articles by, among others, Herbert F. Tucker, Daniel A. Harris, and Carol T. Christ.

A short book that nevertheless provides valuable insights into the poetics of Victorian and Modernist poetry is Carol Christ's *Victorian and Modern Poetics* (Chicago and London: University of Chicago Press, 1984). Christ begins by suggesting that Eliot, Yeats, and Pound, despite an anti-Victorian bias, prolong the tendency toward objectivity inherent in Victorian poetics. They achieve distance through the adoption of personae and masks, the use of objects as images and symbols, and through mythical or historical structures. The relation between the Modernists' use of masks and personae and the Victorian dramatic monologue is analyzed in Chapter 2. The following chapter explores Victorian and Modernist theories of the image as one more way of objectifying experience. Christ shows how Arthur Hallam's definition of the picturesque—a term he applies to Tennyson's poetry—"looks back to Keats and presages Eliot" (p. 55). She notes the combination of feeling with scientific exactitude in the imagery of Tennyson's early poetry, his use of sound, and the ambiguity resulting from the blurring of subject and object; and she relates these features to Eliot's practice in a poem like "Preludes," or Pound's in "Heather." The chapter quotes relevant passages from prominent Victorian critics—John Stuart Mill, Ruskin, Arnold, and Pater—before applying these ideas to the poetry of Yeats, Eliot, and Pound. These poets' use of historical or mythical material is then discussed along with the possibilities inherent in myth as opposed to fictional narrative for structuring a long poem.

Isobel Armstrong's masterful *Victorian Poetry: Poetry, Poetics and Politics* (London and New York: Routledge, 1993) is essential reading for anyone interested in poetry of the Victorian era. It is a comprehensive, thorough, and penetrating study that emphasizes in its analysis of the poetry the links with political and social aspects of Victorian literary life. Indeed, as the first words of the Preface announce, the "poetry and poetics of the Victorian period were intertwined . . . with theology, science, philosophy, theories of language and politics" (p. ix). Conservative and radical political notions are connected with similar trends in poetry. The concept of the "grotesque," for example, is examined for its cultural and political ramifications as well as linguistic ones. Regarding the dramatic monologue, Armstrong rightly identifies its most interesting feature as the duality of focus that enables it to present utterance "both as subject and as object" (p. 13). She emphasizes the sophistication of a form that raises "the problem of its own and the reader's status by confusing speaking, which assumes a listener's presence, with writing, which assumes an addressee's absence" (p. 288). One of several sections on Browning stresses the importance of fiction in his poetry. Apart from the major figures of Browning and Tennyson, whom Armstrong considers from many angles, the book deals with the work of many other poets: Arnold, Clough, Morris, Swinburne, Hopkins, and Meredith, as well as women poets such as Elizabeth Barrett Browning, Christina Rossetti, and less well-known ones such as Augusta Webster, Amy Levy, Letitia Landon, and Mathilde Blind.

## Works on Browning

A good biography of Browning that also includes some pertinent criticism is *The Book, the Ring and the Poet: A Biography of Browning* by William Irvine and Park Honan (New York: McGraw-Hill, 1974).

For the reader interested in Browning's dramatic monologues, a valuable and reliable introduction is Park Honan's *Browning's Characters: A Study in Poetic Technique* (New Haven, CT: Yale University Press, 1961). The first three chapters discuss his earlier works, including the plays. Chapter 4 presents an overview of the dramatic monologue form, and subsequent chapters analyze twenty representative poems of Browning from different perspectives: the speaker and his situation, the audience, imagery, language and diction, rhythm and sounds, and syntax. *The Bow and the Lyre: The Art of Robert Browning* by Roma A. King, Jr. (Ann Arbor: University of Michigan Press, 1957) is another short but useful book for students of Browning. It gives an in-depth analysis of five major monologues: "Andrea del Sarto," "Fra Lippo Lippi," "The Bishop Orders His Tomb at Saint Praxed's Church," "Bishop Blougram's Apology," and "Saul." The final chapter, "The Bow and the Lyre," summarizes the findings of the five commentaries and outlines some general conclusions regarding Browning's poetic techniques and style. Another book by Roma King, *The Focusing Artifice* (Athens, OH: Ohio University Press, 1968) provides an overview of all Browning's poetry. Philip Drew's *The Poetry of Browning: A Critical Introduction* (London: Methuen, 1970) deals with some of the problems involved in reading Browning. He seeks to dispel the notions that Browning was a late Romantic poet and an inveterate optimist.

Isobel Armstrong has edited *The Major Victorian Poets: Reconsiderations* (London: Routledge and Kegan Paul, 1969), a collection of essays on Victorian poets including Browning, Tennyson, Clough, Arnold, and Hopkins. In her own article, "Browning and the 'Grotesque' Style," she comments on the "grotesque" aspect of Browning's style (so named by Walter

Bagehot in 1864), seeing in it a refusal to accept orderly and sequential language because of a desire to present experience, in poetry, as a "whole" or as a process rather than a sequence. Another collection edited by Isobel Armstrong, *Robert Browning* (London: Bell, 1974) includes several interesting essays including Michael Mason's "Browning and the Dramatic Monologue," mentioned above.

J. Hillis Miller's chapter on Robert Browning, in *The Disappearance of God* (Cambridge, MA: Harvard University Press, 1963) focuses on questions concerning language and obscurity in Browning, and also on the notion of the "indeterminacy of selfhood." This fascinating topic has been investigated by more recent critics, such as Warwick E. Slinn in *Browning and the Fictions of Identity* (Totowa, NJ: Barnes and Noble, 1982). His book explores the conflicts and tensions involved in the presentation of the self, as illustrated by Browning's dramatic monologues. By exposing the fallibility of his speakers, Slinn argues, Browning questions the truth of experience and the validity of its expression. Far from seeing the dramatic monologues as a means of achieving objectivity, Slinn regards them as drawing attention to subjectivity and the ambiguities inherent in self-expression.

Loy D. Martin also addresses the conflict in Browning between the desire for unity and the fragmentation and division experienced by the self, as reflected in the language of the poem. His book *Browning's Dramatic Monologues and the Post-Romantic Subject* (Baltimore and London: Johns Hopkins University Press, 1985) is a penetrating and wide-ranging discussion of Browning's dramatic monologues as illustrative of the conflict between the individual and the social forces that mold him/her.

In *Browning and the Modern Tradition* (London: Macmillan, 1976), Betty S. Flowers investigates, as her title suggests, those aspects of Browning's poetry that have been acclaimed by modern poets and that distinguish Browning's work from that of his contemporaries. In particular, Flowers stresses the importance of Browning's adoption of a conversational diction in poetry, and his dramatic method. Among the 20th-century poets she discusses are Yeats, Pound and Eliot, William Carlos Williams, and Gertrude Stein.

Herbert F. Tucker, Jr., adopts a poststructuralist approach in *Browning's Beginnings: The Art of Disclosure* (Minneapolis: University of Minnesota Press, 1980), concentrating on the poet's early works (up to *Men and Women*); he discusses the difficulties inherent in assessing the production of meaning and closure. A recent collection, *Critical Essays on Robert Browning*, ed. Mary Ellis Gibson (New York: G.K. Hall, 1992) includes articles by many of the critics mentioned above, such as Herbert Tucker, Ralph Rader, Warwick Slinn, Loy Martin, Adrienne Munich, and Dorothy Mermin.

## Works on Tennyson

Biographies of Tennyson include Jerome Buckley's *Tennyson: The Growth of a Poet* (Cambridge, MA: Harvard University Press, 1960), and *Tennyson: The Unquiet Heart* by Robert B. Martin (Oxford: Clarendon Press, 1980). Christopher Ricks, editor of *The Poems of Tennyson* (London: Longmans, 1969) has also written a book entitled simply *Tennyson* (New York: Macmillan, 1972) that combines biography and criticism of the poetry. Initially, chapters alternate between narration of episodes in Tennyson's life and discussion of poems and of the relation between the two. After 1855, by which time Tennyson's life was settled (he was married, a father, and Poet Laureate), the book concentrates solely on the remaining works. The criticism is both perceptive and meticulous, including such detailed matters as the use of pronouns in "Tithonus" (pp. 132–33) or the curious avoidance of the future tense in "Ulysses"—a reluctance, "in a poem of such an adventurous setting forth, so strange as to deserve to be called morbid" (pp. 125–26). Ricks does not hesitate to point out negative aspects of Tennyson's verse as well as positive ones. He bemoans the woodenness and complacency of "Tiresias" (p. 135); the lack of feeling created in the reader for either Arthur or Bedivere in "Morte d'Arthur" (pp. 137–39); a note of stridency in "Locksley Hall" (pp. 164–66). In contrast, he admires in "Break, Break, Break" the elusive but suggestive link between the speaker's suffering and the sea's elemental and indifferent force (pp. 143–44); and he praises the "fineness of musical verbalism that makes 'Tithonus' his most assuredly successful poem" and one that is "quintessentially Tennysonian" (p. 131). The discussion in Chapter VIII concerning the problematical questions of unity in *In Memoriam* and Tennyson's relationship with Arthur Hallam is both sensitive and eminently sensible. "Literary criticism since Tennyson's time,"

Ricks declares, "has become more aptly flexible in its ideas as to artistic unity, less committed to a narrow or mechanical idea of such unity. But it has also become more skilled at imagining some such unity, where it may not exist" (p. 212). He draws a parallel with Shakespeare's sonnets, both in respect to the issue of unity and the expression of love for a man. This book is an invaluable guide to any student of Tennyson, expert or beginner.

Linda K. Hughes' *The Manyfacèd Glass: Tennyson's Dramatic Monologues* (Athens: Ohio University Press, 1987) is a very rich and useful study, placing particular emphasis on the dramatic monologues. Hughes provides a sensible discussion of the dramatic monologue form, considers the reasons why Tennyson wrote dramatic monologues, and examines the differences between Tennyson's and Browning's monologues (with respect to the notions of personality and consciousness), concluding that neither poet's "method is superior or inferior to the other; they are simply different" (p. 15). Hughes deals with the issue of the "split" in the dramatic monologue by which the poet becomes both the "Sower and the Seed" (Chapter 2). She fruitfully uses the insight that the action of a dramatic monologue is viewed entirely from within the present of the narrator to illustrate the appropriateness of Tennyson's choice of the dramatic monologue form for "Ulysses" and "Tithonus" (pp. 97–100).

A collection of essays on Tennyson, *Studies in Tennyson* (London,: Macmillan, 1981), edited by his great-grandson Hallam Tennyson, contains articles on different aspects of the poet's work, including one specifically on the dramatic monologues: "One Word More—On Tennyson's Dramatic Monologues" by William E. Fredeman. Fredeman discusses the typical features of nine major monologues by Tennyson and how they differ from those of Browning. Elaine Jordan's *Alfred Tennyson* (Cambridge: Cambridge University Press, 1988) is a general, short introduction to Tennyson's life and works; it includes an interesting chapter on the dramatic monologues, "Monologues and Metonymy." Two additional surveys of Tennyson's poetry are *The Poetry of Tennyson* by A. Dwight Culler (New Haven, CT: Yale University Press, 1977) and Alastair W. Thomson's *The Poetry of Tennyson* (London and New York: Routledge and Kegan Paul, 1986).

It is refreshing to see a whole book devoted to one poem, as in the case of *Tennyson and Personification: The Rhetoric of "Tithonus"* by Daniel A. Harris (Ann Arbor, MI: UMI Research Press, 1986). Harris starts from the basic premise that in "Tithonus" Tennyson is concerned with the process and significance of the act of personification as such—a process that has important theological as well as literary consequences: "Tithonus is revealed to be inventing the Dawn, personifying a phenomenon as a divinity. The poem thus displays theogony not merely as the consequence of human subjectivity but as a linguistic event governed by a rhetorical trope" (p. 2). Harris draws a distinction between the act of personification, by which Tithonus "crafts the Dawn in his own image," and the act of impersonation by which Tennyson takes on the persona of Tithonus (p. 15). The poem provides an example of the dramatic monologue's questioning of the notion of "person." Particularly interesting is the chapter dealing with the Dawn's silence in the face of Tithonus' pleas for release from immortality. She does not reply for three reasons: as Tithonus' personification and as the auditor of a dramatic monologue, she *cannot* speak; as a Divinity (in Tithonus' view), she *will* not. These three explanations embody different aspects of the poem: Tithonus' psychological weakness, in asking for release from a phenomenon he has himself deified; the formal characteristics of the dramatic monologue; and the process of theogony. This is not an easy book, but it will interest the student who already has some knowledge of Tennyson and wants to focus closely on the issues raised by a single poem.

The question of mortality in "Tithonus"—and, to a certain extent, in "Ulysses"—is discussed by W. David Shaw in "Tennyson's 'Tithonus' and the Problem of Mortality," *Philological Quarterly*, 52 (1973), 274–85. Shaw's book, *Tennyson's Style*, (Ithaca, NY, and London: Cornell University Press, 1976) provides invaluable insights into the stylistic features of Tennyson's poetry, though relatively little space is accorded specifically to the monologues.

Alan Sinfield, in his short book *Alfred Tennyson* (Oxford: Blackwell, 1986), devotes a whole chapter to "The Politics of Poetry," insisting on the social and political context of Tennyson's poetry and of poetry in general. He also deals with issues such as subjective identity and the continuity of selfhood, and the related questions of language and style (Tennyson's "ornate" style, in Walter Bagehot's terminology).

143

## Works on Ezra Pound

As Christine Froula points out in her Introduction to *A Guide to Ezra Pound's Selected Poems* (New York: New Directions, 1983), many readers find Pound's poetry inaccessible without some explanation of his allusions, startling images, and disconcerting juxtapositions. In addition to notes on individual poems, a short introductory paragraph is provided for each one, placing it in a spatial and temporal context. The general Introduction to the book outlines the main stages of Pound's poetic career. The book covers selections from Pound's *Cantos* as well as his early poetry, notably the poems contained in the 1926 edition *Personae: The Collected Poems of Ezra Pound*, including the *Homage to Sextus Propertius* (1919) and *Hugh Selwyn Mauberley* (1920). A similar commentary on Pound's poetry is provided in Peter Brooker's *A Student's Guide to the Selected Poems of Ezra Pound* (London: Faber and Faber, 1979). K.K. Ruthven's *A Guide to Ezra Pound's Personae* (Berkeley and Los Angeles: University of California Press, 1969) covers all the early poetry but not the *Cantos*.

Hugh Witemeyer's *The Poetry of Ezra Pound: Forms and Renewal, 1908–1920* (Berkeley and Los Angeles: University of California Press, 1969) provides an interesting and thorough account of the development of Pound's poetic technique and an excellent discussion of his early works. Witemeyer uses Pound's prose writings to shed light on the poetry, and he stresses the continuity of Pound's poetics and thought throughout his career. The first two chapters examine his place within literary tradition and his attitude toward that tradition, as well as his poetic theory. Chapter 4 analyzes several individual poems from *Personae*. Pointing out that these poems often constitute "a rather transparent mask for Pound himself," Witemeyer argues that "Pound's personae . . . are exercises in historical imagination and also in creating a vivid personal identity" (p. 60). The book discusses the early poetry up to and including *Hugh Selwyn Mauberley* and is highly recommended for the student of Pound's early poetry.

For anyone wishing to look beyond the early works and explore the *Cantos*, the best introduction is *Ezra Pound and the Modern Verse Epic: The Tale of the Tribe* by Michael André Bernstein (Princeton, NJ: Princeton University Press, 1980). This book discusses the *Cantos* as an epic, that is "a poem containing history," as Pound himself puts it; a poem whose audience is the *citizen* rather than the individual, and that is narrated not so much by the individual voice of the poet, but apparently, by the voice of "the community's heritage 'telling itself'" (p. 14). Although Pound's own voice can certainly be heard, especially in the Pisan Cantos, "far more sections of the poem are simply given, generated with no locatable or definable narrative source" (p. 171). In his desire to write the "tale of a tribe," Pound shares with Browning a leaning toward mimesis, narrative, and historical subjects. The *Cantos* evoke the actions, attitudes, and utterances of a multitude of historical figures, famous and obscure, ancient and modern; Bernstein declares that, as "an extended poetical treatment of history in which the data of scientists, anthropologists, and statesmen could figure, *The Cantos* are, quite simply and literally, unique" (pp. 31–32). This book also discusses two other "modern verse epics," William Carlos Williams' *Paterson* and Charles Olson's "Maximus" poems.

James Knapp's *Ezra Pound* (Boston: Twayne Publishers, 1979) provides a brief but thorough examination of Pound's entire career, beginning with the early poems of *Personae*, discussing his ventures into Imagism and Vorticism, his discovery and use of Chinese poetry, his concern with social issues, and the form and content of the *Cantos*.

Resemblances and differences between the dramatic monologues of Pound and Browning are examined in Christoph N. De Nagy's essay "Pound and Browning," in *New Approaches to Ezra Pound: A Co-ordinated Investigation of Pound's Poetry and Ideas*, ed. Eva Hesse (London: Faber and Faber, 1969). The article discusses the "Browningesque" poems in *Personae*, for example, "Piere Vidal Old," "Cino," "Marvoil," "Sestina: Altaforte," and "Villonaud for this Yule."

## Works on T.S. Eliot

Eliot was determined to keep his private life private, wanting to maintain the distinction between "the man who suffers and the mind which creates," as he puts it in "Tradition and the Individual Talent." Much of his personal correspondence is still unavailable to researchers. Nevertheless, Peter Ackroyd, in *T.S. Eliot* (London: Hamish Hamilton, 1984), has explicitly made "the connection between the life and the work," as he promises in his "Prelude," and has produced a very readable and interesting account of Eliot's largely uneventful and often unhappy life. Many photographs of Eliot, his relatives, and friends enliven the text. Another biographical study is Lyndall Gordon's *Eliot's Early Years* (Oxford and New York: Oxford University Press, 1977). This book provides both an account of Eliot's life and a discussion of his works through *The Waste Land*, including some of the youthful, unpublished poems. Gordon focuses—justifiably—on the religious strain in these early works, emphasizing the continuity of this theme in his poetry.

A classic work forming an excellent introduction to the poetry of T.S. Eliot is Hugh Kenner's *The Invisible Poet: T.S. Eliot* (New York: McDowell, Obolensky, 1959). Kenner takes the reader chronologically through Eliot's works, with minimal biographical detail, concentrating on elucidating and interpreting the texts. There is a chapter on Laforgue, one on Bradley's philosophy and its relation to Eliot's poetry, one on the essays, and some discussion of the drama, especially *Murder in the Cathedral*; but the main emphasis is on the poetical works. The book is written in a very readable, lively style, with many quotations in support of the author's comments. The title reflects Eliot's recommendation for the "invisibility" or impersonality of the poet.

Ronald Bush examines the question of Eliot's impersonality in his *T.S. Eliot: A Study in Character and Style* (New York and Oxford: Oxford University Press, 1983). Eliot often advocates an impersonal poetry; yet, as Bush points out, every statement of Eliot's regarding the need for the poet's "impersonality" can be countered with one recommending that poetry should give "the undertone, of the personal emotion, the personal drama and struggle," as Eliot says in his essay on John Ford (*Selected Essays*, 180). Bush's book assumes that, in the last resort, poetic voice is inseparable from character and seeks to discover the connections between the two—recognizing, meanwhile, that "character" is often elusive or contradictory. The chapter on rhetoric indicates the link between duplicity of language and insincerity born of social conditioning, and stresses Eliot's emphasis on emotional honesty and his "need to assert a life deeper than the poses of rhetoric" (p. 44). Bush seeks to elucidate the link between Eliot's inner life, in this sense, and his poetic style. His book is by no means a biography but a detailed and thoughtful account of Eliot's poetic development from the satire of social posturing in his early verse to the more musical and "symbolist" poetry of *Four Quartets*; it provides a sensitive analysis of the poetry, especially from *The Waste Land* onward.

In *T.S. Eliot's Silent Voices* (Oxford and New York: Oxford University Press, 1989), John T. Mayer reads Eliot's early poems as the product of the "silent voices" of the psyche. He makes a distinction between the dramatic monologues of Browning, and Eliot's psychological monologues or "psychologues." Browning's voices express "fixed personalities with fixed world views," whereas Eliot's "record feelings and awarenesses" (p. 12), giving us the thoughts rather than the speech of the persona. Hence the "sharp breaks and discontinuities that baffled 'Prufrock's' earliest readers" (p. 10)—though one might object that Browning's earliest readers were similarly baffled by the twists and turns of his one-sided dialogues. Each chapter of this book examines a group of poems—beginning with the early, unpublished works from Eliot's Harvard years—from the point of view of voice, role-playing, the quest for identity, and the inner life of the consciousness and of the unconscious. Chapter 3, "Pierrots and Roles: Voices Within," discusses Eliot's early poetry in relation to that of Jules Laforgue. "Portrait of a Lady" and "Prufrock" are analyzed at length in Chapter 5, "Playing at Relationship." The book ends with two chapters of discussion on *The Waste Land*.

## Works on Robert Frost

One of the best introductions to Frost is William H. Pritchard's *Frost: A Literary Life Reconsidered* (New York: Oxford University Press, 1984), which offers a combination of biography and criticism; a whole chapter is devoted to *Mountain Interval* and *New Hampshire*. Pritchard concentrates largely on elements of voice in Frost's poetry: his dry humor, his "homely" speech, and what Frost calls the "sound of sense."

Richard Poirier's *Robert Frost: The Work of Knowing* (Stanford, CA: Stanford University Press, 1977), provides a sensitive and comprehensive study of Frost's poetry. Poirier analyzes most of Frost's major poems and some neglected ones, such as "A Star in a Stoneboat." The excellent initial discussion of Frost's early poetry is followed by a chapter dealing with the concept of home and the values and traumas associated with it in his poems. These comments are particularly relevant to "A Servant to Servants" as well as to other poems pitting husband against wife, such as "Home Burial," "The Death of the Hired Man," and "The Fear." Another chapter centers on the issue of time, the seasons, and moments in time; and one deals with Frost's politics and his reputation vis-à-vis Eliot and Pound. Poirier also discusses the design and form of Frost's poetry, his use of sounds and of metaphor. This is still one of the best critical works available on Frost.

An interesting and very readable general guide to Frost's work is *The Poetry of Robert Frost*, by John Robert Doyle, Jr. (Johannesburg: Witwatersrand University Press and New York: Hafner, 1962). The author begins by picking out the most salient features of his poetry and in subsequent chapters examines selected poems as illustrations of these aspects of his work. He discusses Frost's use of description and the dramatic characteristics of his verse, tone, themes, and ideas. He also notes the importance of the lyric impulse in Frost's poetry, which tends to be neglected because of the popularity of his more dramatic works. The final chapters provide a short biography of Frost and a discussion of his work in relation to that of other modern poets. Mordecai Marcus' *The Poems of Robert Frost: An Explication* (Boston: G.K. Hall, 1991) examines all of Frost's works, in chronological order; and Judith Oster's *Toward Robert Frost: The Reader and the Poet* (Athens and London: University of Georgia Press, 1991) analyzes selected poems by Frost while exploring the relationships among reader, poet, and text.

Two interesting articles relate specifically to "A Servant to Servants." Stuart B. James, in "The Home's Tyranny: Robert Frost's 'A Servant to Servants' and Andrew Wyeth's 'Christina's World'" (*South Dakota Review* I, No. 2 (1964), 3–15) discusses images of the American home as a "dwelling place of guilt, sorrow, and death." The author gives an extended analysis of "A Servant to Servants" and draws an interesting parallel between the poem and Andrew Wyeth's picture, "Christina's World." Constance Rooke's "The Elusive/Allusive Voice: An Interpretation of Frost's 'A Servant to Servants'" (*Cimarron Review*, 38 (1977), 13–23) provides a detailed analysis of "A Servant to Servants." Particularly interesting is the discussion of the importance of the natural world to the protagonist, and of her husband's attitude towards her.

## Works on Randall Jarrell

In *Understanding Randall Jarrell* (Columbia: University of South Carolina Press, 1986), J.A. Bryant provides a short and clear guide to Jarrell's works for the benefit of students, as part of the series *Understanding American Contemporary Literature.* A brief introduction concerning some of the ideas and symbolism in Jarrell's works is followed by chapters devoted to the early poetry, the essays and criticism, his novel and children's stories, and the later poetry. Another short but thorough and well-documented survey of Jarrell's life and works is Sister Bernetta Quinn's *Randall Jarrell* (Boston: Twayne, 1981). It contains a useful Selected Bibliography of books and articles on Jarrell.

*The Poetry of Randall Jarrell* by Suzanne Ferguson (Baton Rouge: Louisiana State University Press, 1971) offers a clear and interesting analysis of the most significant poems of Jarrell's poetic career. She stresses the dramatic and narrative tendencies in Jarrell's work; he is a poet who "projects his feelings and ideas as representative of common rather than individual experience" (p. 3). The book is illustrated with photographs of Jarrell, his family, and friends.

Students of contemporary poetry suffer from the disadvantage that very little critical work is available. No full-length studies have been written on Richard Howard; he is barely mentioned even in the recent *Columbia History of American Poetry*, ed. Jay Parini (New York: Columbia University Press, 1994). However, this paucity will encourage the student to do what should of course come first with any poet—to become thoroughly acquainted with the poetry itself before turning to criticism.

Most of the works mentioned above contain bibliographies that may lead to additional readings, if desired.

# Recommended Reading

This list of recommended dramatic monologues is arranged alphabetically by author.

## Robert Browning

The following dramatic monologues can be found in annotated editions of Browning such as *Robert Browning: The Poems*, Vol. 1, ed. John Pettigrew (New Haven, CT, and London: Yale University Press, 1981); or *The Poetry of Robert Browning*, ed. Jacob Korg (Indianapolis: Bobbs-Merrill, 1971). Many other selections of Browning's poetry are available, with and without notes, and most of them contain many, if not all, of the poems in this list.

Browning moved some of his poems from one volume to another. The poems listed below are grouped according to the collection in which they now appear, and the original publication date of each collection is given.

From *Dramatic Lyrics* (1842):

"My Last Duchess": Probably Browning's most famous and most frequently discussed dramatic monologue. Browning very cleverly makes the speaker unwittingly reveal, through his own words, his haughtiness and self-importance.

"Count Gismond"

"Soliloquy of the Spanish Cloister": As its title suggests, this poem is not addressed to an auditor. The speaker is monk, who reveres the letter of the law more than the spirit.

"Porphyria's Lover": The speaker addresses his dead lover, Porphyria, shortly after strangling her with her own hair. The poem illustrates a common feature of Browning's dramatic monologues: a preference for dramatic incidents and reprehensible characters.

From *Dramatic Romances and Lyrics* (1845):

"Pictor Ignotus"

"The Bishop Orders His Tomb at Saint Praxed's Church": The poem analyzed in Chapter 2.

"The Laboratory": A dramatic monologue spoken by a woman consumed by jealousy and addressed to a pharmacist; he is preparing a poison with which she intends to get rid of her rival.

"The Confessional": A Spanish woman curses the Catholic church: She once confessed her love life to a priest; he persuaded her to tell him about her rebel lover's secrets, in order to "save his soul," and a few days later she witnessed his execution. Like the previous poem and many others, this poem exemplifies Browning's preference for highly dramatic situations.

From *Men and Women* (1855):

"Up at a Villa—Down in the City": An "Italian Person of Quality" rhapsodizes about the advantages of city life.

"Fra Lippo Lippi": Fra Lippo is caught out at night by the watch; he speaks to justify his womanizing and to defend his views on art— which resemble those of Browning. The poem is one example of Browning using a speaker to present his own ideas.

"A Toccata of Galuppi's"

"Saul"

"An Epistle Containing the Strange Medical Experience of Karshish, the Arab Physician": This monologue takes the form of a letter, from Karshish to his master, Abib. The epistle is probably the oldest form of dramatic monologue. Writing a few years after the death of Christ, Karshish relates, with simultaneous incredulity and fascination, the story he has heard of the resurrection of Lazarus.

"Cleon": Another epistle-poem, again concerning religion and written not long after the death of Christ. The writer, Cleon, who is in search of spiritual fulfillment, concludes from hearsay that the Christian doctrine "could be held by no sane man." Both this poem and the previous one rely for their effect on the hindsight that, for the reader, lends a certain irony to the pronouncements of Karshish and Cleon.

"A Serenade at the Villa"

"'Childe Roland to the Dark Tower Came'": A much-discussed and very ambiguous monologue. Does Childe Roland succeed in his quest or does the end of the poem enact a failure? The quotation "Childe Roland to the Dark Tower Came" is from *King Lear*.

"Master Hughes of Saxe-Gotha"

"Bishop Blougram's Apology"

"Andrea del Sarto": One of Browning's most successful and moving dramatic monologues. The painter, Andrea del Sarto, has betrayed his artistic ambitions in order to paint popular, "faultless" pictures that, however, lack genius. He does so to earn money to please his wife, whom he loves above all else but who nevertheless betrays him. The pathos of the poem derives from the fact that he is aware of his own failings but is too weak-willed to take decisive action. The Italian background is clearly rendered.

From *Dramatis Personae* (1864):

"Abt Vogler": A monologue in which the speaker's enthusiasm for his music takes precedence over characterization. It is written in a less colloquial style than most of Browning's dramatic monologues.

"Rabbi Ben Ezra": A Rabbi muses on youth and old age, life and death.

"Caliban upon Setebos; or, Natural Theology in the Island": Caliban, the man-monster from Shakespeare's *The Tempest*, muses in his primitive way about the nature of God. The God he worships, Setebos, is cruel and stupid like himself. The "Natural Theology" of the poem's subtitle refers to a theology based on natural phenomena, without revelation. As in "Fra Lippo Lippi," Browning is often considered to be presenting his own views through Caliban, though there is some disagreement as to the exact import of Caliban's pronouncements.

"Mr. Sludge, 'The Medium'": A medium defends himself against accusations of fraud. Spiritualism was a controversial topic in Browning's day, and a subject of discord between Browning and his wife. This is the only poem of Browning's set in the United States.

*The Ring and the Book* (1868): A series of very long dramatic monologues presenting the viewpoints of different characters concerning the same issue: the guilt or innocence of Pompilia, charged by her husband Count Guido of adultery with a priest. This work cleverly exploits one of the chief features of the dramatic monologue—presenting experience through the inevitably biased view of an individual—to show the difficulty of knowing objective "truth."

*Prince Hohenstiel-Schwangau, Saviour of Society* (1871): A long poem in which Napoleon III, exiled in England, muses on historical events and on his own career. The poem presents the anomaly of being a soliloquy addressed to an interlocutor—who turns out to be a figment of the speaker's imagination.

## T.S. Eliot

Eliot's dramatic monologues can be read in *Collected Poems of T.S. Eliot 1909–1962* (New York: Harcourt, Brace and World, 1963); or *Collected Poems 1909–1962* (London: Faber and Faber, 1963). They also appear in many selections of Eliot's poetry, and in anthologies.

From *Prufrock and Other Observations* (1917):

"The Love Song of J. Alfred Prufrock": Probably the most famous dramatic monologue of the twentieth century. The setting is of a social gathering in an upper-class drawing-room. Prufrock displays a typically twentieth-century self-consciousness in his social life, particularly his relations with women. The poem is a soliloquy, addressed by Prufrock to himself.

"Portrait of a Lady": the poem analyzed in Chapter 3.

"Preludes"

"Rhapsody on a Windy Night": Both this monologue and the previous one are primarily descriptive of the outer world—a world of "sordid images."

From *Poems* (1920):

"Gerontion": An old man muses about his life and times.

*The Waste Land* (1922): Dedicated to Ezra Pound, "il miglior fabbro," who had given Eliot much advice on making cuts in the poem. *The Waste Land* won the $2,000 Dial Award. It represents a kind of collage of dramatic monologues with passages of dialogue, with different speakers and varying meters. It was one of the most influential poems of the twentieth century.

*The Hollow Men* (1925): A monologue in the first person plural expressing the sense of hollowness apparent in the title, and groping toward religion.

*Four Quartets* (1943). Not dramatic monologues, though written in a somewhat impersonal first person. Interesting to read as a contrast to the dramatic monologue form—as well as for their value as Eliot's supreme masterpiece.

## Robert Frost

Frost's poems are available in *The Poetry of Robert Frost,* ed. Edward Connery Lathem (New York: Holt, Rinehart and Winston, 1969).

From *North of Boston* (1914):

"A Servant to Servants": This poem is examined in Chapter 4, and it appears to be the only one of Frost's poems that conforms strictly to the dramatic monologue form, though many of his other poems are more dramatic than lyrical in inspiration. Some are in dialogue form, such as "Home Burial" and "The Death of the Hired Man" from *North of Boston,* or "Snow" from *Mountain Interval.* "The Bonfire" (*Mountain Interval*) is a dramatic monologue with three lines of dialogue spoken by the audience (children). Some of his poems, such as "Mending Wall" (*North of Boston*) and "The Exposed Nest" or "Christmas Trees" (*Mountain Interval*) read like dramatic monologues with countrymen or farmers as speakers—but this persona is indistinguishable from that of the poet, since he lived on farms for a large part of his life.

## Zbigniew Herbert

From *Selected Poems,* trans. Czeslaw Milosz and Peter Dale Scott (Penguin Books, 1968):

"The Return of the Proconsul"

"Elegy of Fortinbras": Spoken by Fortinbras to the dead Hamlet.

From *Report From the Besieged City and Other Poems,* trans. John Carpenter and Bogdana Carpenter (New York: Ecco Press, 1985):

"The Divine Claudius": The Roman Emperor reviews his life and defends himself against accusations of wanton cruelty.

"Damastes (Also Known as Procrustes) Speaks": He, too, tries to justify the cruelty of his actions. Both these dramatic monologues have political overtones that are valid for the twentieth century.

## Richard Howard

From *Untitled Subjects* (New York: Atheneum, 1969), which won the Pulitzer Prize for 1970; the titles of these poems—many of which are dramatic monologues—are often simply dates. To fully appreciate them, and other poems by Howard, the reader needs to know a little about the speaker's life.

"1825": The speaker is Sir Walter Scott.

"1851, A Message to Denmark Hill": A letter from Ruskin, in Venice, to his father in London.

"1824–1889": An apostrophe to Wilkie Collins, who was born in 1824 and died in 1889.

"1915, A Pre-Raphaelite Ending, London": The dramatic monologue discussed in Chapter 4.

From *Findings* (New York: Atheneum, 1971):

"November, 1889": A long dramatic monologue, set in Italy, spoken by
Browning a few days before his death, and addressed to his son
Pen and Pen's wife Fanny. Browning died at Pen's palazzo in
Venice in December 1889.

From *Lining Up* (New York: Atheneum, 1984):

The section entitled "Homage to Nadar" (a famous nineteenth-century French photographer) contains several
"inverted" dramatic monologues addressed to, rather than spoken by, famous nineteenth-century French painters, writers and
musicians, such as Delacroix, Millet, Corot, Berlioz, and Michelet,
complete with their photographs.

From *Like Most Revelations* (New York: Atheneum, 1994):

"Poem Beginning with a Line by Isidora Duncan": A dramatic monologue spoken by the dancer Isidora Duncan.

"Visitations": A woman married to a German psychic medium and
speaking to a doctor in London's famous Harley Street seeks to
reassure herself about her powers of sexual attraction.

This volume, as well as many of Howard's other collections, also contains poems that are not strictly dramatic monologues but experi-
ment with the form. Some poems are addressed to a named figure, rather than being spoken by him or her; sometimes Howard
addresses himself by name. Many poems are in dialogue form.

## Randall Jarrell

His monologues may be found in *Complete Poems* (New York:
Farrar, Straus and Giroux, 1969)

From *Selected Poems* (1955):

"The Truth"

"The State": Many of Jarrell's early poems concern World War II. These
two monologues show the reactions of two children to the way
the war has affected their lives.

From *The Woman at the Washington Zoo* (1960), winner of the National
Book Award:

"The Woman at the Washington Zoo": This splendid dramatic monologue catches the essential truths about an individual woman but
is also typical of many twentieth-century women's lives.

*A Sad Heart at the Supermarket: Essays and Fables* (1962): Contains an essay
on the poem "The Woman at the Washington Zoo."

From *The Lost World* (1965):
"Next Day"
"The Lost Children." Both this poem and "Next Day" concern, again, the
everyday lives of women speakers.

## Rudyard Kipling

Kipling's verse is available in *Rudyard Kipling: The Complete
Verse*, ed. M.M. Kaye (London: Cathie Kyle, 1990), and in-
cludes dramatic monologues such as "McAndrew's Hymn,"
"Mulholland's Contract," and "The 'Mary Gloster.'"

## Robert Lowell

His dramatic monologues may be found in *Lord Weary's Castle;
and The Mills of the Kavanaughs* (San Diego: Harcourt Brace
Jovanovich, 1979); or in *Poems 1938–1949* (London: Faber and
Faber, 1950)

From *Lord Weary's Castle* (1946), which won the Pulitzer prize for poetry:
"Mr. Edwards and the Spider"
"After the Surprising Conversions": Both these monologues are spoken
by the eighteenth-century Calvinist Jonathan Edwards, whose
sermons dwelt on hellfire and eternal damnation.

From *The Mills of the Kavanaughs* (1951):
"Mother Marie Therese": A Canadian nun remembers her eccentric former Superior, Mother Marie Therese, who drowned in 1912. The
poem reveals aspects of the very different characters of the nun
and of Mother Marie Therese.

## Edgar Lee Masters

His *Spoon River Anthology* (New York: Macmillan, 1944) is a collection of dramatic monologues, also available in an annotated edition, ed. John E. Hallwas (Urbana: University of Illinois Press, 1992).
*Spoon River Anthology* (1915): All the poems in this collection are short
dramatic monologues, spoken from beyond the grave by the
inhabitants of the imaginary town of Spoon River.

## Czeslaw Milosz

Milosz's *Collected Poems 1931–1987* (London: Viking Press,
1988) contains dramatic monologues such as the "Songs of
Adrian Zielinski," set in Warsaw during World War II.

## Ezra Pound

Pound's dramatic monologues appear in *Personae: The Shorter Poems of Ezra Pound*, ed. Lea Baechler and A. Walton Litz (New York: New Directions, 1990); and in *Selected Poems 1908–1959* (London: Faber and Faber, 1975).

From *Personae* (1909):

"La Fraisne": As in most of Pound's dramatic monologues, the speaker is a Provençal troubadour, Miraut de Garzelas, who is said to have run wild in the woods, crazed with love. Pound attempts to give the impression of an unbalanced mind by the use of ellipsis points and disconnected fragments. The poem is composed in free verse but not in the colloquial tone of many of his dramatic monologues.

"Cino": The troubadour Cino walks the open roads reflecting on his life and his art. He has loved and sung songs to women, but they prefer men of greater social standing. So, he decides, he will "sing of the sun." The poem is written in a highly colloquial, Browningesque style and catches the verve and *insouciance* of Cino's attitude.

"Marvoil": The poem analyzed in Chapter 3.

"Na Audiart": The troubadour Bertran de Born, spurned by the lady he loves, constructs in revenge an ideal lady in this poem, which manages to convey simultaneously a spirit of playfulness and a sincere expression of love.

"Sestina: Altaforte": A dramatic monologue in the elaborate "sestina" form. This poem presents another side of Bertran de Born's character: the warlike nature of a "stirrer up of strife."

"Piere Vidal Old": This poem presents the speech of a man who ran mad, as a wolf, in the mountains.

"Ballad of the Goodly Fere": Spoken by Simon Zelotes after the Crucifixion, this is the only one of Pound's dramatic monologues not set in Provence. The poem resembles a Scottish ballad in its rhythm, vocabulary and elisions of consonants (for example, "I ha' seen him drive a hundred men/Wi' a bundle o' cords swung free . . .").

## Edwin Arlington Robinson

His monologues may be found in *Collected Poems* (New York: Macmillan, 1937).

From *A Man against the Sky* (1916):

"Ben Jonson Entertains a Man from Stratford": The man from Stratford is a friend of Shakespeare's. In this blank verse monologue, Ben

Jonson expresses a somewhat puzzled admiration for Shakespeare, who manages to succeed even while breaking all the rules of drama established by Aristotle.

From *The Three Taverns* (1920):
"The Three Taverns": Spoken by Paul on his way to Rome to see Caesar.
"John Brown": Shortly before his death, John Brown addresses his wife, regretting the bloodshed he has caused in his fight for the abolition of slavery.

From *Avon's Harvest* (1921):
"Rembrandt to Rembrandt (Amsterdam, 1645)": The painter addresses himself, deploring the reception of his paintings by his contemporaries but defending his conception of art.

From *Nicodemus* (1932):
"Toussaint l'Ouverture (Chateau de Joux, 1803)": Toussaint, imprisoned in the fortress of Joux, reflects bitterly on his struggle with France for the freedom of blacks in Haiti.

## Allen Tate

Tate's *Collected Poems 1919–1976* (New York: Farrar, Straus, Giroux, 1977) contains several dramatic monologues, including "Lycambes Talks to John (in Hell)," "To the Lacedemonians," "Aeneas at Washington," and "Aeneas at New York," all written in the 1920s and 1930s.

## Lord Alfred Tennyson

Tennyson's dramatic monologues can be found in *The Poems of Tennyson,* ed. Christopher Ricks (London: Longmans, 1969); *The Poetical Works of Tennyson,* ed. G. Robert Stange (Boston: Houghton Mifflin, 1974); or any reasonably complete edition of Tennyson's poetry.

From *Poems* (1832; dated 1833):
"Oenone":Virtually a dramatic monologue, but with a short narrative introduction.

From *Poems* (1842):
"Ulysses": Having returned from Troy, after many years on the high seas, Ulysses announces to his fellow sailors his decision to leave Ithaca once more. His spirit of adventure is so strong that he feels bound to leave his country, his wife, and his son. Critics have

debated whether we are to criticize Ulysses for this decision or admire him for his courage and integrity.

"Saint Simeon Stylites": In this poem Tennyson satirizes the Saint's mortification of the flesh in the name of religion.

"Tithonus": Analyzed in Chapter 1. This poem contains many examples of the melodious verse for which Tennyson is renowned.

"Locksley Hall": The speaker returns to a scene of his youth, Locksley Hall, and recalls his love for his cousin Amy, who loved him too but married, at her parents' insistence, a "clown." He bemoans the social pressures that cause such loveless marriages—a common theme in Tennyson—but also berates Amy for her faithlessness.

*Maud: A Monodrama* (1855): Another poem on the theme of lost love, this is a long work divided into three parts. Part I has twenty-two subsections and Part II five, all in varying meters with different stanza-lengths. The speaker is clearly unbalanced, possibly paranoiac, as a result of the loss of his beloved Maud, whose brother he killed in a duel, after which she died of grief. Tennyson pointed out that in this poem "different phases of passion in one person take the place of different characters," and indeed the poem presents a fascinating and highly-developed psychological study. It was one of Tennyson's most popular poems in his day.

From *Enoch Arden, etc.* (1864):

"Northern Farmer (Old Style)"

"Northern Farmer (New Style)": These two poems are written in Lincolnshire dialect in a style that is therefore very unlike Tennyson's usual elevated, poetic diction. The sense of humor manifest in the poems is also unusual in Tennyson's verse.

From *Ballads and Other Poems* (1880):

"Rizpah": A dying woman bewails her son's death by hanging, for robbery. She had collected his bones and buried them in a churchyard.

"In the Children's Hospital": A sentimental poem spoken by a nurse in the children's hospital. Tennyson is often accused of sentimentality, though not usually in the dramatic monologues.

"The Northern Cobbler": Another dialect poem.

From *Tiresias and Other Poems* (1885):

"Tiresias"

"Despair": The speaker, after a failed suicide attempt, attacks Calvinist doctrine and expresses the pessimism to which it has led him. His views on Calvinism coincide with those of Tennyson.

From *Locksley Hall Sixty Years After, Etc.* (1886):
"Locksley Hall Sixty Years After": Published forty-four years after "Locksley Hall," this poem was much less successful than the earlier one, being somewhat hysterical in tone. It presents the opinions of an older man looking back on his youth and addressing his grandson.

## Louis Untermeyer

Untermeyer's *Selected Poems and Parodies* (New York, Harcourt Brace, 1935) includes several dramatic monologues, such as "Eve Speaks," "Moses on Sinai," and "Monolog from a Mattress," spoken by Heine.

# Index

# The Author

Before beginning her academic career, Elisabeth A. Howe worked as a linguist at the United Nations in Geneva and for the British government. She speaks French, Russian, and Polish. She received a Ph.D. in Romance Languages from Harvard University in 1987 and currently teaches French and Comparative Literature at Assumption College in Worcester, Massachusetts, where she is an Associate Professor. She has published a book on the dramatic monologue in French literature: *Stages of Self: The Dramatic Monologues of Laforgue, Mallarmé and Valéry*, which won the NEMLA/Ohio University Press Book Award for 1989. Her articles on French poetry have appeared in journals such as *French Forum, French Review, Nottingham French Studies,* and *The Comparatist.*